Moyo means **Heart** (Translated from Swahili)

It has also been described as meaning **Heart, Life and Spirit**.

This book is about listening to your heart, learning from your life

and connecting with your spirit so you can live your life more authentically.

~

This book is dedicated to all Inner Travelers™

who are courageously taking their Inner Journey

to discover the power of listening to their own heart

~

With gratitude to my son

who inspires me to live my life authentically,

to be fully present and to not make excuses.

Thank you for challenging me to

take action and stop talking,

claim my voice and gifts

and to shine my light

in the world!

I love you

with all my moyo!

Momma

I have discovered on my journey of life that there are angels who appear to give us priceless gifts we could not have imagined. One of my angels is Jack Presnal, founder of the Community Film Studio Santa Barbara.

He was looking at my manuscript and having seen my show, he said, "This all sounds like inner travel to me." He also said, "You might want to take a look at other languages like Swahili in particular to see if there is something that resonates."

That is how I received the perfect word and the branding for my first Inner Traveler's™ Guidebook. Thank you for your wisdom and generous Moyo Jack.

ASANTE SANA means **Thank you so very much!**

Another angel on my journey to writing this book has been Karl Grass. aka "Luigi".

Karl is a coach and author of <u>Compassion Haikus: Daily Insights and Practices for Developing Compassion for Yourself and for Others</u>.

After hearing my CD *Love Your Self*, he said, "Linda, this sounds like the book you've been writing. Have you thought of making each song a chapter?"

Karl, your support and encouragement have inspired me to keep listening to my heart and to continue creating and birthing that which is inside of me.

Grazie!

There are many more angels and travel guides to thank. Please see pg. 212

Moyo

Discovering the Power of Listening to Your Own Heart

Linda Newlin

Design and photography: Annie Gallup, Julie Hayes Nadler, Wendy Drasdo, Jack Presnal, Linda Newlin

Original cover painting by: Nancy Taliaferro

Editorial Review: Alice Chaffee, Annie J. Dahlgren

Images contained within this book were purchased at 123RF Stock Photos Compasses, Maps, Sundial, Coffee Drink, Ocean Spyglass, Clouds 7882883, 13109895, 13542944, 10906202, 11058586, 9351784, 10482437, 11245558

Printed in the United States

Library of Congress Cataloging-in-Publication Data
LCN Number: 2013901030

Luna Madre Publishing
    The Inner Traveler's™ Guidebook To: Moyo

Newlin, Linda and Luna Madre™ Music
    CD Music - *Love Your Self: The Musical Journey Home*™ © 2012

ISBN: 978-0-9887724-4-1

LUNA MADRE.COM

Guiding
INNER TRAVELERS
to emerge and become
shining lights in the world

How did this Book/CD/Musical come to be?

I was working with a Somatic Coach in 2009, to get clear about where I wanted to focus my coaching and speaking career. She asked me to **Listen To My Heart** and the words *songwriting* came out.

I guess I lit up while saying my heart's desire and when I opened my eyes, she said. "I hope you're musical." I laughed and said, "I used to be, but had given up music 25 years before."
Upon leaving my session, I had a chat with myself that went like this:

> "I don't have time to song write.
>
> I need to make money. End of chat."

Fast forward two years and I am teaching a new leadership course and I hear myself saying, "Listen to your heart's desire and do what lights you up." (Oh no – here comes the old Indian name for tonight – "Me Hypocrite")

I went back to my room that night and picked up a pen and paper and said, "Ok, I'll try this songwriting thing." And in ten minutes I wrote the lyrics to my first song and CD titled **Love Your Self.**

I had to laugh out loud at my resistance to doing what my heart had told me to do two years before.

So I said, **"OK then, if it just takes ten minutes, I guess I do have time."** ☺

So from here I had to begin the next phase of the journey home. I had to **Forgive Myself** for not acting upon and honoring my heart's message. I had to write another **Song To Self,** which brought me to the understanding of how I abuse myself by ignoring my inner voice and keeping myself from being truly happy.

I began to declare that **It's Not Okay** to keep investing in others' dreams and not my own. I began to see that what I was looking for **Over The Rainbow** was inside of me. I was a pot of gold with gifts I didn't use.

I had allowed some **Crazy Makers** in my life to create doubt in my abilities and connection to my inner wisdom and guidance. I had fallen off my path of creativity. But the words kept coming *"no more excuses"* and *"I forgive myself for trusting the words they would say."*

Each song that came through had the guidepost to what healing was next. I then began to hear the familiar words to my favorite childhood song play in my ear and I decided it was time to listen and take heed to my voice and callings.
I had to love myself enough to express what was being given to me for my own healing path and let **This Little Light of Mine** shine in a whole new way.

As I began to write and record these songs, I was filled with joy that I had not felt since the birth of my son. I started to change physically and I felt so youthful and happy. There was a flowing vitality and fire within me. From this place of aliveness and enthusiasm, I had to claim and declare who I truly was at this point in my life. So my anthem for this part of the journey was **The Woman I Am**.

I can't describe what it was like to be divinely inspired with the words to these songs. They were such a gift to me and helped me to heal and change. I then started seeing visions of ways to share this. The universe aligned with my vision and I met Kate Wallace and Deborah Wynne, the composers of the music, and David West who opened his magical studio to me. From there, came the stage show *The Musical Journey Home* and now <u>Inner Traveler's Guidebooks</u>.

How do you explain this kind of synchronicity?

Listening to my own heart has been the key.

When our passions/gifts/purpose are in alignment, the universe can help open the doors to make things happen that couldn't otherwise. That's the only explanation I have for the miracles that have happened in less than 18 months since I first put pen to paper.

I had never written a song before, and yet as I connect and write, it is the easiest and most natural thing. It is who I am.

I realized it was my HEART telling me to be even more of myself now…songwriter, author and performer! It's what lights me up now! I am just beginning to experience how listening to my heart is key for my fulfillment and fullest expression of why I came to this planet.

And it's never too late to know and express all of who we are. One day my son was telling someone that I had just made my first CD and was doing a stage show. He said, "You know, it's never too late, even if you are a winter chicken."

The next day, he said, "You know, Mom, I've been thinking. You really aren't a winter chicken, you're really a summer chicken." I have a few more seasons left! Thank goodness ☺

This book is a musical exploration and healing journey to discover what your heart wants and to explore what might be keeping you from living your authentic and peaceful life.

It is also a journey to discover what is inside you that wants to EMERGE and heal so you can BECOME more of who you truly are so YOU CAN SHINE YOUR LIGHT IN THE WORLD!

Happy Trails and Blessings on your Journey Home to YOU!

When I was a little girl, we moved quite often. I remember one of the rituals we had was writing goodbye letters to our friends when we were leaving. The letters were always filled with HOPES and WISHES for a safe journey and what we wished for them when they got to their new military home.

So I close this part of the introduction with my letter to you, *dear inner traveler:*

I hope that you listen to your heart and act on your heart's desires.

I hope that you are gentle and compassionate along the way.

I hope that you will reach out for help/support when you need it.

I hope that you laugh out loud and release all your tears of grief.

I hope that you experience great wonderment and surprises along the pathways and vistas you will encounter.

I hope that you give yourself the gift of being who you truly are.

I hope that you end all forms of suffering that you are experiencing.

I hope that you find joy and love beyond your wildest dreams.

I hope that you share your "growth" and healing with others.

I hope that you invest in your dreams NOW. (It's never too late!)

I hope that you find forgiveness and freedom from past hurts.

I hope that you claim your wholeness, lovability, strength and wisdom.

I hope that you find what lights you up and shine it in the world!

I hope that you experience bliss, passion and pleasure as never before

I hope you live an authentic and passionate life.

I wish you deep peace.

Linda

<u>Welcome to the Musical Journey Home!</u>

This book includes the music and lyrics from my CD Love Your Self.

As you journey through you will encounter opportunities to listen to the songs, reflect and write about your life's experiences.

*You will find **EXPLORATIONS** and **PRACTICES** to support your inner journey.*

<u>*Travel Essentials for Your Inner Journey*</u>

1. *You*

2. *The Music (p.14)*

3. *Your Inner Travel Guidebook To Moyo*

<u>*Helpful Inner Travel Companions*</u>

1. *Your Curiosity*

2. *Your Courage*

3. *Your Compassion*

4. *Your Favorite Chocolate! or Coffee drink*

No suitcases required for Inner Travel

Overture

I had learned about self-love and listening to your heart in the very first book I read at age 12. I have listened to speakers, teachers and workshop leaders talk about how important it is to follow your heart and to *Love Your Self*. I am a teacher of this practice. And…very much still a student.

When my clients/students tell me "you're such a great teacher, *I Let My Guard Down* and always say, "That's because I'm still a darn good student." And indeed my life is filled with continual learning opportunities and new dimensions of listening to my own heart and deepening my own self-loving compassion.

I thought I was living my dreams and had felt that I followed my heart throughout much of my life. What I didn't know until now is that I had ignored my heart more times than I had listened to it. I did not truly love myself fully.

I had not followed the hunches, urges, warning signs and red flags that my heart was trying to guide me with, along my life's path. When I chose not to listen, it had to communicate somehow.

I shiver at the cosmic 2x4s that I have endured because I wasn't listening. Just a few wake up calls I've experienced: Hit by four drunk drivers in twenty months, 9/11, multiple miscarriages, a near death experience and divorce.

Nothing like pain to wake me up. This inner journey is about learning to listen and heal that which isn't working in your life, so you can end your suffering and truly express your whole self and shine your light in the world!

Here is my disclaimer:

I do not have the answers.

I do know that **you have the answers within you,** and I hope that the music and writings created for this Inner Journey take you to a place of clarity, freedom, wholeness, peace, self-love and self-expression of who you truly are.

What does your heart want? It's *Time to Go Home* and Discover for Your Self!

To Download Your 13 mp3 Song Files

From Love Your Self CD

http://lunamadre.com/music_download.htm

Why do we ignore our internal messages, hunches, urges, gut feelings?

Why do we have a "story telling critical committee" inside our heads ruining our very peace of mind and telling us lies about who we are?

Why do we talk ourselves out of the things we want to do?

Why do we talk ourselves into things we don't want to do?

Why do we give ourselves away to organizations, people, addictions and other distractions and not live our dreams?

Why do we lose connection with our passions, gifts and desires?

Why do we go along with what others want for us and not stay true to ourselves and follow the path we want?

Why do we stay in relationships that aren't healthy or nurturing?

Why do we tolerate abuse of any kind? (Emotional, physical, financial)

Why do we abuse ourselves? (Critical self talk, negative thinking, ignoring our dreams, giving ourselves away, addictions)

Why do we suffer in silent and not-so-silent ways?

Why do we pretend to be happy when we are not?

Why do we give up?

Why?

One possibility is that we were taught to do so.

OK and…even if we learned to ignore our hunches, intuition, and heart…Why would we keep doing these things if they don't work for us in our life?

Because the things we learned to do in childhood have been our survival strategy.

Bob Hoffman developed a theory 45 years ago and created a healing program that addresses what he calls the "Negative Love Syndrome." He believed that as human beings, we need our mother's and father's love and approval to survive and get our needs met. If a child does not get the unconditional love and acceptance she needs, she then has to adopt mother's and father's patterns, traits, beliefs and ways of being in order to get the love. Our very survival depends on it.

It's as if the child has to say, "See I'm just like you, now will you love me?"

We not only adopt the positive traits, beliefs and values of our parents to get their love and approval….we take on their negative patterns, affects, moods, emotions, physical movements, attitudes and ways of being in the world.

This means we may become more like them than our authentic selves right from the very beginning of our life journey.

These negative patterns we adopt can show up in our lives in three ways:

> 1. We do the pattern to ourselves.
> 2. We do it to others.
> 3. Others do it to us.

So let's say you had critical parents…you could end up in your life:
1. Being critical of yourself.
2. Being critical of others.
3. Others in your life being critical of you.

Patterns keep us from living in the present. They can run and ruin our lives. We want to be authentically ourselves. We want love, connection and freedom, and yet our patterns create the opposite effect.

Sadly, we often don't recognize how these patterns are running automatically until such time as we become parents. We then start hearing ourselves say things to our kids we swore we never would. We find ourselves reacting in ways our parents would.

Bob Hoffman found that patterns typically show up in our intimate relationships most vividly because that is where we learned them. Some people keep finding that they are in a relationship with their "mother" or their "father" and can't break a pattern of a certain type of partner. Some find themselves working for a boss who is just like their mother or father.

Bob's theory suggests that, "Whatever you got in childhood is what you equate with love. So if being judged and needing to be perfect were what you equate with love, you will continue to attract people who judge you and encourage you to be perfect. Or you will be attracted to people who need you to judge them and encourage them to be more perfect. Fixing others may be another pattern born out of the dynamic you had in childhood."

So if it feels like love, smells like love, looks like love…. it must be love.

And it might feel just like your childhood experience (if you selected with your unconscious patterns).

<u>What did I learn about love in my childhood?</u> *Some possible examples: Love is about pleasing others, saving others, lying to myself, pretending I'm happy, going along with things, not rocking the boat, giving up my dreams, making others happy, tolerating abuse/addictions, ignoring needs, working to give what others want.*

<u>What did my parents' model/teach me about listening to my heart and following my inner guidance to live an authentic, peaceful and passionate life?</u>

Bob's healing program is called the Hoffman Quadrinity Process™ and he founded the Hoffman Institute over 45 years ago. It is now offered in more than 13 countries around the world. It is not marketed like other "transformational" workshops that you are familiar with. It was his belief that when someone is ready to find their way home to their authentic self and "spirit" and stop living with and acting out their parents' patterns, they will find the Process.

I was fortunate that my dear cousin David found the Hoffman Process in 1993. When he returned from his eight-day intensive workshop, he looked different. And indeed he was different. As he described to me, "You know what I've been searching for my whole life, I have finally found it inside myself."

That's all I needed to hear. I signed up without knowing anything more. That is ONE significant moment I listened to my own heart quite easily when it said, "I want that for myself." This was the beginning of my deep healing.

While I was at Hoffman, I had a memory arise that gave me such clarity about my "patterns" of trying to prove myself and please others.

When I was in the womb, my parents thought they were having a boy. Before I even was born, I was already developing unconscious strategies about how I was going to prove that I was OK and that they shouldn't be disappointed since I was indeed a girl. Basically I imprinted an adopted belief that I was the wrong sex. I began wondering what I could do to get them to love me before I was out of my mother's body.

When I was born the first words I heard were "Oh, I'm sorry Mrs. Newlin, the plumbing fell off. It's not a football player, it's an opera singer." My mother told me this story as well. Is it any wonder I didn't accept myself fully and be who I truly was?

20

I felt that I needed to be perfect to be loved for much of my life until I found the healing gift of the Hoffman Process.

I had another memory of hearing my mother talking to a friend one day while I was in utero. The conversation went something like this. "I don't really care what this baby is, I just hope it sleeps."

Bingo…that is one thing I can do to get love and approval. <u>Sleep.</u>

Apparently my sister, who was born before me, was a terrible sleeper and colicky. So another "adaptation" I could take on was to be a solid sleeper.

This pattern becomes quite significant as my journey unfolds and you'll learn why sleeping was a behavior that would harm me in my later years.

AND

As a metaphor for "being asleep" to my own needs…my own callings…the red flags…the inner wisdom that I needed to be listening to.

As I began to look at my life patterns, I discovered that I had been ruled by a number of beliefs that turned out to be both false and harmful. In this Inner Traveler's Guidebook you will see how I've used these EXPLORATIONS to lead you through the journey of self-discovery. They are written as negative false beliefs.

I have replaced these with self-loving practices that have led me to the truth **that the more I love myself; the more I can give to others.**

Our Soul
Is
Found
Through
Subtraction

The soul is reached through subtraction, not addition.

This journey is about discovering the things that can be subtracted, so you can find your Moyo – Heart/Life/Spirit. By becoming authentically you, you can live a peaceful, purposeful and passionate life.

There are many pathways to self-love, self-compassion and listening to your heart. Within these pages are some of the specific tours; landmarks, destinations, experiences, routes and pathways I had to travel in order to do the **subtraction** work and find my way back home.

I have included some life experiences of other travelers along the way to provide examples and insights from places I had not journeyed through.

For male travelers reading this, I have attempted to keep the language as broad as possible so that you can experience the journey as it resonates with you.

It is my hope that this Guidebook supports your Inner Travel to help you find the answers within yourself and truly discover the power of listening to your own heart.

Listen To My Heart

Here we are
You and I at last
In the right place
At the right time
Every dream
I've dreamed has come to pass
Cause you're right here
And you're all mine

I can't believe the years of holding back are through
And I can finally share what's in my heart with you
Listen, listen, listen to my heart
Listen to it sing
Listen to my voice
It wants to tell you everything
There's so much to say
I don't know where to start
but if you want to know the love I'm feeling
Listen to my heart

All my life
I've been on a road
Going one way toward one dream
The road would wind and down it I would go
Always searching
Never finding

But even in my darkest hour I always knew
That someday somehow the road would lead to you

And words can't express
How my heart's filled with happiness

Listen to it
Listen to my heart, listen to it sing
Listen to my voice, it wants to tell you everything
Listen to my song
Listen to it soar
I've waited all my life for this one moment
I'm not waiting anymore

Listen to my heart
As it cries
For all the years
That it was lonely

Listen to my heart
As it smiles to know, that now after so long
I can finally sing my song
And you're here and you're listening, you're listening

Listen to my voice and it will tell you everything
All about the life
That's just about to start
For if you want to know how much I love you
Listen to my heart, Listen to my heart
Listen to my heart

Words and Music by: David Ball & Allen Shamblin

When I first heard this song I was sitting in a creative workshop taught by Alexander Tolken, and I found myself singing every word out loud and crying tears of joy. I had never heard or seen the words to this song before and yet somehow I knew them all.

I felt a vision of myself standing on a stage singing this song to an audience and joy filled my whole being. I knew in that moment that I was supposed to sing this song and share my gifts in a way I had never done before.

Sometimes there is no explanation.

Sometimes when we try to put words to our experience it loses the magic and impact.

Sometimes we have no idea why we are so moved by something and what our future holds.

Sometimes our hearts speak to us in words, sometimes through music, sometimes through nature, sometimes through pain.

As I wrote my first song, "Love Your Self," I had no idea it would turn into a musical and a book.

I also had no idea what healing would come from my reclaiming my whole self and my gifts that I had hidden away. I stopped singing when I was 21. I started singing again when I was 40.

Why?

The answer lies in the pages to come.

As I shared with you in the introduction, I thought I was following my heart most of my life. It wasn't until I began that fateful day in 2009 when I actually took the time to go into my heart space and ask specific questions that I began to uncover the power of listening and acting upon my heart's desire.

Proactively asking and following my own inner guidance from my heart has proven to be miraculous and life affirming.

It has also required my courage and compassion.

<u>Listening was just the first step</u>.

<u>The second step was actually taking action on what I was hearing</u>.

As you know I didn't take action on the songwriting message for almost two years.

After having the first song come so easily, I had to explore why I wasn't taking action more quickly and look at my resistances.

As I began the journey, I also had to realize that I had created some challenges and roadblocks throughout my life by not listening and ignoring my heart's messages. Self-forgiveness is a travel companion you will want for your journey.

The good news is that it's never to late to get started and to change!

For now, let's begin your journey by asking this question of your heart.

One way to listen to your heart is to breathe into your heart space and take your whole self into that space of your heart and ask…. Then listen.

It may be words, images, sensation, feelings or song titles that communicate the message from your heart. Receive it in the way your heart delivers it.

What gifts within myself have I not expressed fully or have put away?

What patterns/beliefs/roadblocks have hindered me from expressing these gifts?
(What did my parents do about fully expressing their own gifts?)

Notice what you experience and how it is to listen to your heart.

Be curious and open to how you find your way into your "listening" and connection to your heart.

Take your time if it feels like you're not receiving anything. This may be the very first time you have consciously asked your heart directly for answers to your questions.

For those of you who are more experienced inner travelers, you may have a different way of connecting with your heart.

> **Now is a good time for me to make more disclaimers as we embark on this Muziki Safari** (musical journey).

My intention of this book is to share my personal journey and experience in a way that will inspire Inner Travelers to emerge from any past limitations and become more fully who they are and shine their lights in the world.

Your journey will be different than mine.

It is my hope that you find what resonates with you at this point in your life and that the words evoke action to become more fully who you are by listening to your own heart. I answered the call from my heart to song write and I am continuing to follow my heart into writing guidebooks.

Becoming more fully who I am and expressing myself is the greatest fun and grandest adventure I've ever been on. I wish you the same outcome!

Thank you for joining me as I share with you the words that my heart cried out so I could heal and learn to love myself with compassion and grace.

POSTCARDS
From My Inner Journey

Lying in my crib...
Praying to the Powers Above
Help me to help them

Love Your Self

Lying in my crib
Wondering how to help them
Praying to the powers above
Help me to help them

Lying in my bunk bed
Wondering how to change them
Pleading with the powers above
Help me to change them

Why do they drink so much?
Why do they yell so much?
Why can't they help themselves?
Are there any magic spells?

Lying in my queen size
Wondering how to save them
Begging to the light above
Help me to save them

Lying in my grave now
Couldn't save them anyhow
The ones I loved who hurt so much
Still the powers above gave me a loving touch

Wasn't your job to save them
Next time love yourself and pray for peace, Amen

Lyrics By: Linda Newlin ©2011

"What do you mean? Wasn't it my job to save them? If I don't who will?"

"Yes, I hear you… I understand the words you're saying, however, I don't quite think it's possible for me to give up and stop trying to save the people I love."

"Yes, you're correct. I didn't exactly save them. I just keep trying to save them."

"I hear the words and conceptually I understand that they need to help themselves and it's not my responsibility."

BUT…

"Yes, you're correct."

"I spend a lot of my time focusing on others and not on my own life."

"It has made me feel useful."

"I have been the good person I am supposed to be."

"Yes you're correct."

"I have not used my own gifts fully as I've been focused on helping others."

"So are you saying that I might be of more use to the people I love and to the world, if I were to save myself and invest in my own gifts?"

"What if I become and express who I am supposed to be and not just what I perceived others need me to be?"

OK. I hear the words and it makes sense to me.

However, my first reaction is 'I don't think I can do that.'

I can't put myself first as that feels selfish.

I then remembered a coach years ago saying to me, "Put yourself first on the list" and I said, "What? I'm not even on the list." (That's how bad it was.)

So I had to ask myself:

Why was I so resistant to putting myself first on the list?

The answer was not that clear and it took me a while to actually discover all the ways I was resistant. After some time, I decided to ask my heart why I was so resistant to being first on the list.

"Because I don't want to be selfish."

Good answer, I thought!

BUT… WELL… AND …

"The Bible teaching something about our neighbors, the kindergarten teacher who told me to share, my role models of self sacrificing…
Being selfish was not an option. So if self-love is not selfish, then what?"

I realized at this point that there was much more to explore. The explorations in this book are presented as the negative beliefs we may have about what self-love and compassion really are.

Exploration #1
The belief that self-love is selfish

Being a writer, I know that the use of words and what they mean can be quite helpful in discovering certain insights about my beliefs.

So off to the Webster's Dictionary I went to look up Self-love.

OK, hold on to your suitcase…

Webster's notes:

> **Self-love**
>
>> **Egotism**
>>
>> Synonyms: **Conceit, self-centeredness, narcissism, pride, vanity, selfishness, arrogance**

OK then. That's settled.

My negative belief #1 is true then.

Can we stop writing songs about this and go home now?

My heart said, "Not so fast."

Exploration #2
The belief that self-love is narcissism

It's pretty hard to love yourself if it's not about you.

Yes that's true.

But it can't be about me.

And then I saw the dilemma I've struggled with inside myself for years.

It couldn't be about me because I don't want to be a narcissist.

I had experienced narcissism and was just beginning to learn more about it. What I did know was that I was afraid of being selfish and didn't ever want to be narcissistic.

So this did indeed seem like a good place to stop the pursuit of self-love and get off the plane.

My heart said, "Wait, there's more to it and you just can't stop now."

Exploration #3
The belief that self-love is helping others first/rescuing

One fateful day, I had to explore my third belief about self-love from the airline's perspective.

I was traveling to Hawaii with my young infant son and the flight attendant did her "emergency talk" and she walked right up to me and said, "Did you hear what I said about the oxygen masks?"

I said, "yes."

She then proceeded to say, "You need to put your mask on first and then help your son."

I was slightly offended and then she said, "You look like the type of mother who doesn't get the point of this. ***If you don't help yourself first, you'll die and be of no use to him.***"

OK then. I think I heard you loud and clear.

Truth be told, I understand the concept of why you should put your oxygen mask on, but hadn't been confronted with the reality of my automatic responses until that moment. There would be no way I would put my mask on first and then do my child's mask.

And then my heart said, "Resist your resistance. You could possibly lose both your lives because you insist on doing it your way."

Back to the first page of this chapter:

What could I lose if I don't save myself first?

My very life, it seems (and possibly those I love).

To this day I'm grateful for that flight attendant who confronted me and helped guide me to where I am today. From this new vista I began to ask even more questions:

What if I gave to myself first in my life?

(My journey seems to take me right where I need to go, while I'm exploring).

I went to a parenting workshop a few weeks later and the speaker talked about how if we don't teach our children to love themselves, they won't learn it anywhere.

She then pointed out that when we lose patience and get resentful it's a sign that we aren't taking care of ourselves enough.

Here comes that "coach's advice" again. Put yourself first on the list. YIKES

My heart said, "Just try it."

<u>Self-loving practice #1</u>
Put yourself first on the list

As I pondered how I might try this first practice, I remembered seeing a diagram at the Hoffman Process that was a cup of love. They had a definition of self-love that had something to do with "filling your own cup first" so you could give from a whole and complete place.

Unconditional love arises from that full space within you.

I liked the concept and believed it was a good idea, but I wasn't good at doing it. I hadn't learned much about healthy self-love from my parents.

I had learned about self-sacrifice, martyrdom, the messiah complex, and hidden narcissistic behaviors, which can be very confusing and it was not clear what unconditional love and healthy self-love really was.

And my parents learned very little about self-love from their parents and the generations that came before them.

<u>I was a traveler</u>
<u>without a self-loving compass within myself.</u>

<u>Time to review the Travel Guide</u>:

If self-love is not selfish, self-sacrificing, rescuing, and narcissistic, then what is it?

I was just beginning to experiment with the simple practice of putting myself first on the list once in a while to see how it felt.

Little things (that will make you laugh), but felt huge at the time.

I started letting myself finish brushing my teeth if my son called for me (and it wasn't an emergency). He could wait ten seconds and I could complete.

I told you that you would laugh!

Now it seems absurd, but you get the picture of how bad I was at it.

Then I graduated to "I get to pick where we eat tonight."

And then to the next step, "I'm going to get a babysitter so I can go to a movie that I want to see."

Baby steps were the pathway for me.

What amazed me in the experimenting was how bad I felt about putting myself first. I knew I had some more exploration to do in this regard.

Fortunately one of my travel guides helped me to see the source of my guilt and difficulties with putting myself first. I was afraid to be selfish and narcissistic.

If I was first, then I was like the people I swore I'd never be like.

This led me to do more research on the fear of being narcissistic.

I had to educate myself and understand the differences between unhealthy self-absorption and real self-love. It finally became clear that self-love is NOT narcissism.

I will recommend a couple of travel guides about narcissism:

The Wizard of Oz and Other Narcissists, by Eleanor Payson.

Will I Ever Be Enough? by Maryl McBride

After reading these books, it became clear why I had a lot of resistance and misinformation.

I asked my heart for guidance at this point.

"Resist your resistance. Keep exploring."

<u>Self-loving practice #2</u>
Resist your resistance

My heart encouraged me to look a little deeper and travel a little farther into the words of Webster.

Within a few miles, I reached the definition of **Pride:**

> **Self-love, delight, dignity, happiness, honor, pleasure, joy, satisfaction, self-regard, self-respect, self-trust, self worth**

Might all this be possible for me if I could stop saving others and actually love myself in a healthy way?

If I could love myself, then might I feel delight, happiness, joy, satisfaction?

43

That sounds great. I'll sign up for that tour.

But somehow I didn't know how to get on board that healthy pride train.

So I started reading other books about self-love and self-compassion.

I gleaned from the books that: **Self-love is the key that unlocks the door to freedom, wholeness, joy, peace, fulfillment, purpose and magnanimous loving relationships."**

And I started to believe that **Self-love could create peace in the world**.

All that resonated on some level for me and I also recognized that I didn't have a framework for executing it for myself.

One of the ways I learn besides reading is by observing.

I started watching people around me who appeared to love themselves (put themselves first) in a healthy way…And I saw that they had loving fruitful relationships, they were not selfish, narcissistic, egotistical, used, abused, or taken advantage of, they weren't suffering, they were thriving, and they were happy and healthy. They were kind to themselves and others.

I noticed that their whole family was balanced, joyful, caring, loving and they were contributing to their world. Seeing and watching them in action gave me a model for how it could look in my future.

It helps to have a vision of what you want.

And I was just beginning.

Reflections

<u>Who have I tried to save or whom am I still trying to save?</u>

<u>What has been the cost to me and to them?</u>

What might be possible if I stopped rescuing others?

What did I learn about self-love in my childhood?

<u>What was it like for me to not be seen, heard and acknowledged for being uniquely me?</u>

<u>How hard is it for me to see, hear and acknowledge myself now?</u>

<u>What self-loving things do I do for myself now?</u>

<u>What things do I wish I were doing for myself now?</u>

<u>Some additional exercises if they apply and feel useful at this time:</u>

Write a letter to the person(s) you've been trying to save and tell them how hard you've been working to help them and how hard it is to watch them suffering. Say it in the way you've always wanted to say (no holds barred)…

Acknowledge any "messiah" savior need in yourself that you are aware of:
(Note who you learned to "save others" from in childhood)

And then with compassion and love, commit to channeling that energy into saving yourself and freeing yourself from any suffering that you are experiencing in your life right now.

<u>Permission Slip</u>

I hereby grant permission to myself:

_____

Your Name

To put my oxygen mask on first

To stop rescuing others

and

To learn more about self-love and compassion

If you were taught to "rescue" others and try to save others, then possibly deep within you is the _**desire to be rescued**_.

I was doing both things. Rescuing and hoping to be rescued.

Growing up with Hollywood's image of the Knight in Shining Armor and the Prince on the White Horse fed my share of fantasies operating deep below the surface of my rational mind. (For men it's saving the Damsel in distress, fighting to the death, rescuing her from death.)

The image of what romantic love was going to look like is dreamy and idealistic. (According to Walt Disney's version of what love will be.)

What I was learning was that our need for love is a basic human need. And by our teen years, we start to turn outside the family to get the love we need and want.

I grew up with what I perceived as a non-fantastical and unromantic model for love and I thought I was a worldly well-traveled, educated teen. I was not aware of my own deep hidden dream of being rescued.

Quite honestly, it mainly showed up in my life as I was rescuing the other.

As I wrote this next song, I had to come to terms with my outdated and dysfunctional "fantasies" of how love was going to be.

**I warn you …**

**It isn't pretty!**

Let My Guard Down

It was a new Ford truck
A white princely horse
That drove up to my heart
And swept me off course
He knew how to kiss
And he knew how to dance
He carried me to be
And I slept in his trance

He talked a good game
Sang a beautiful song
Danny, angel was his name
How could this be wrong?
I truly believed him
When he whispered in my ear
"You're being loved
By the best my dear"

I thought he loved me
But he used me
Why oh why
Did I hang around?
He fooled me
He seduced me
I was dumb enough
To let my guard down.
Dumb enough
To let my guard down

He flipped overnight
Once he knew he had me
Jekyl turned to Hyde
And treated me so badly
The pain began to flow
I cried myself awake
I remembered what I know
That fairy tales are fake

chorus

This was no prince charming
I'd been taken and been played
The vampire Danny, angel
Sucked me dry
And flew away

Oooh he used me
Oooh why oh why
Oooh he fooled me

I was dumb enough
To let my guard down,
I let myself down
Dumb enough
To let my guard down.

Lyrics By: Linda Newlin © 2011

OK, I told you it wasn't pretty.

But I am grateful for the "wake up" call that this relationship gave me. This was just one of the "princes" I fell hard and fast for. There have been a few like this.

So my need to rescue and help others combined with my "fantasies" of being rescued were a lethal combination.

First, I had to let go of my dreamy programming of "my prince will come" and that with just his kiss; he'll save me from death. I didn't want to…as getting swept off my feet was a fantastic feeling and a worthy life quest for prince charming himself. I was not easily swayed into thinking this was a bad pursuit.

It wasn't until I had near financial ruin, multiple heartbreaks, sheer exhaustion and pain that I was even willing to look at the possibility that this fairytale wasn't working for me.

In speaking with male travelers, I realized that having boys grow up to look for a damsel in distress and make her his princess is also not helping our relationship success quotient.

And then we have the more modern new age pursuit of our Soul Mate.
I must admit I'm still hoping for that one… I can give up on the white horse… but my ONE AND ONLY?   Well that's a stretch. ☺

All kidding aside… these fairy tales and mythology are not serving any of us in relationship land. They all have to go because they aren't working.

And there's nothing like pain or loneliness to tell us things aren't working.

Heart Like a Wheel

Some say a heart
Is just like a wheel
When you bend it
It can't be mended

And my love for you
Is like a sinking ship
And my heart is on that ship
Out in mid ocean

When harm is done
No love can be won
I know this happens frequently

And I can't understand
Oh please God hold my hand
Is why this had to happen to me?

And it's only love
And it's only love
That can wreck a human being
And turn her inside out

Lyrics and Music by: Anna McGarrigle

Yes, love can wreck a human being and turn them inside out.

Why is it that often when our hearts are broken we go into all the wonderings of how we could have "saved it" or made them love us still? We often turn ourselves inside out.

<u>We don't ask self-loving questions like:</u>

>*Was this really working for me?*
>*Was I able to be myself fully with him/her?*
>*Did he/she really love me for who I was and did they want what I want?*

I realized that at a very core of my being was this DRIVE to do whatever I could to make someone else happy and hoping that they would want to be with me.

I had to figure out who they wanted me to be and I'd be so flexible I'd do whatever they wanted.

Turning myself into a pretzel.
Becoming a chameleon.
Forcing myself into clothing styles and hairstyles they wanted.
Becoming someone I was not.

Some of the crazy things we might do when we're in love:

- Ignore the warning signs
- Change physically for them
- Choose things they want
- Do things we don't like
- Pretend we're happy
- Stay trapped/be trapped

- Work out like crazy
- Move and sell everything
- Give up our religion
- Go without sex
- Allow abuse/disrespect
- Deny our hopes/dreams

<u>What are some of the crazy things I have done for love?</u>

In reflecting upon this I realized how I had sacrificed my dreams for someone else's. I even sold all my belongings to live on a sailboat (and I get sea sick). What was I thinking?

Love is not just blind...I've discovered it can also be deaf, dumb and a bit crazy!

What has been the cost for turning myself inside out for love?

I realized in answering these questions that I have adopted the belief and practice that I had to **WORK FOR LOVE**...

<u>Ways I have worked for love that weren't self-loving/self-compassionate:</u>

I had tried every strategy:

> Run after them, do all the work for both of us, move thousands of miles away to be with them, sell my belongings, give them my money, work so they could have what they wanted materially and live in the houses they wanted.

And I lost myself.

I sacrificed what I wanted and who I was.
I would go along with them.
All the while telling myself that I was enjoying it.

My heart just wanted to hear them say:

> "You're the one I've been waiting for."
> "You're not like all the others I've dated"
> "I've wanted to find someone just like you."
> "I can't wait for my parents to meet you"

Exploration #4
The belief that self-love is giving up who I am in order to be loved by you

What parts of myself have I given up along the way?

What dreams have I given up in order to make others' dreams come true?

Exploration #5
The belief that self-love is making others' dreams come true

There is a subtle distinction and balance between real partnership and love…healthy give and take…
AND
Self-sacrifice, giving up dreams, pretending you're happy (while barfing)…

I had them slightly askew.

It is in the realization that I had given up my own dreams that I began to question what is a healthy balanced relationship.

I had experienced something different in my business…when I did what I loved and committed to my dreams, I attracted others who were wanting the same dream. It was supportive and all were fulfilled as they got to be who they were in the business also. So I knew it was possible to co-create mutually beneficial and magnanimous enterprises.

That was just not my operating system for my love life.

What was missing in my love relationships? Me, myself and my authentic dreams.

I didn't realize for decades that I was not being truly authentic with those I loved. I had learned as a child to be a chameleon and please others.

I was not "wired" to ask:

> What's in this for me?
> Does this work for me?

I believed that would be narcissistic. So I was not going to do that.
I was programmed on a deep unconscious level to be wanted by someone and to become what they wanted me to be so they would love me.

No wonder I was attracting CRAZY MAKERS.

I was driving myself crazy with my dysfunctional ways of "abandoning myself."

Exploration #6
The belief that self-love requires that I abandon myself

I do remember right after college a therapist saying to me, "You need to spend a year all by yourself, Linda. And then when you start dating, I want you to ask yourself this question while on the date:"

'Do I want to date you again?'"

I laughed at first…but a year later was faced with the reality that this was going to be difficult for me.

The first date I went on, the guy said, "I can't wait for my mother to meet you."

(Hook, line and sinker)…

He's singing my old song, "If he wants me, I'm in."

Fortunately, I got back to my senses—and to my therapist—before I walked down the wrong aisle.

She then helped guide me into a deeper quest into these questions:

<u>What did I have to do as a child to get love?</u>

<u>Who did I have to be?</u>

What was I wanting and longing for in relationships?

What needs have not been met in my relationships?

How might I be abandoning myself in my relationship today?

What was my parents' relationship like?

Thank God for therapists! Where else can you go and talk for fifty minutes and have someone listen to you?

Side note: As a child I was offered money to not talk…so that gives you a good perspective on the level of *extrovertedness* I naturally possess.

All talking aside… I am most grateful for all the ones I've been fortunate to have healed with.

Through no fault of my gifted therapists, I thought I was making progress in my healing journey and letting go of my fantasies of finding Mr. Right…

When suddenly I fell madly in love with Mr. Unavailable.

When I heard the song ***Heart Like A Wheel***, written by Anna McGarrigle, I found a new piece of the puzzle. I realized that I was like a ship sinking out on the ocean, as I loved someone I couldn't have.

I then began to wonder why I had often been attracted to people who were not really available emotionally or physically through long distance or circumstance.

I then realized the source of this negative love pattern.

My father was in the military and was gone for significant times in my early years. So love was about "not being there."

I had an imprinted belief system: **that people who love me aren't there for me.**

And so I was not there for myself.

I decided to take time for myself to heal.

"There are cracks in everything.

That's how the Light gets in."

~Leonard Cohen

Thank goodness our hearts do heal.

<u>Self-loving practice #3</u>
Work with a Coach

With time, and more coaching, healing, and journaling, I learned more about what I needed to subtract to develop more self-loving practices and a vision of finding healthy love.

The support of a coach took me to the next vista.

Notice if you have any resistance to having support and help from a coach.

We often learn we have to do it all by ourselves and we miss out on the very thing we need/want most. Support for our journey.

With new knowledge and armed with commitment to do things better, I began to love myself more and listen to my heart.

I then met someone who seemed like no one I had met before.

I was convinced I had broken my patterns and finally gotten it right this time.

This was my soul mate. The one I'd been waiting for.

CRAZY MAKERS

What in the world
Is happening here?
I think I'm losing
My mind I fear

Nothing seems
To make any sense
The fog I'm in
Couldn't be more dense

What in the world
Are you saying now?
You didn't say that
And I'm wrong somehow?
You say one thing
And you do another
Always blame me
Or my mother

Crazy Makers
Never take the blame
Crazy Makers
Will drive you insane
Crazy Makers
Never say I'm wrong
How crazy am I
To have stayed so long?

I'm gonna hang
A video recorder
With a tiny microphone
In the corner
Gonna catch your
Narcissistic act and see
You're the Crazy Maker
My friend, not me!
Oh no, no, it's not me

Done drinking the punch
And being out to lunch
Not gonna miss you
I have a hunch
Leave you alone
On crazy island
Sail away and keep smiling!

Crazy Makers
Never say I'm wrong
I've had enough Crazy Makers
So long
So long
I've had enough
So long
Crazy Maker
So long
I'm gone

Lyrics By: Linda Newlin © 2012

Crazy Makers!

What was I thinking?

How did I end up on this lonely confusing island?

Where was my guidance system?

How did I miss the red flags?

I thought I knew better!

The litany of shaming myself was long and deep.

After beating myself up, I finally came up for air and found solace in the fact that I had finally left crazy island and I could see why I had stayed so long.

Confusion kept me stuck for years.

The rollercoaster had some wonderful highs to carry me through the wild turns and ups and downs.

It was crazy to stay that long.

Why did I stay so long?

Because it felt like love, smelled like love.

Some qualities Crazy Makers can exhibit:

Say one thing and do another - False promises

Image focused

Selfish/Jealous/Want others to be jealous of them

Lack of empathy

Blaming others for what happens and their reactions

Alludes to "you are the crazy one"

Dr. Jekyl - Mr. Hyde personality flips

Forget what they said/did - "I never said that".

Lies/Denies/Criticizes

Teflon – no responsibility for actions

Prefer life to be fun and may not like to work that much

Say mean things and minimize your hurt feelings

Control what you wear, how you speak, want to fix you physically

Deny they want to control you/accuse you of controlling behaviors

Entitled/break rules and act superior or above the law

It's best if things are all about them/you are better off going along with them

Project their "negativity" onto you

Won't own their part of a conflict – remain cold/unemotional/or rageful

Threaten suicide or to leave you if you don't…or if you leave them.

Isolate you from your long-term friends, family. Possessive.

Erratic behaviors: drive recklessly to scare you, test your "love" for them

Silent treatment (sometimes for days). Silence is violence

Raging, physically abusive, verbally abusive, emotionally abusive

Exploration #7
The belief that self-love is making it OK for others

I was trained as a child to make it OK for those I loved.

This was a huge revelation for me. And certainly, if I had been able to love myself before this, I am guessing I would have been able to recognize the things I was "normalizing" as not OK and moved more quickly to safe territories.

In discovering more about what the broad range of crazy-making behaviors are I discovered I had more of them in my life than I realized.

Who are the crazy makers in your life right now?

What would be possible if you stopped making it OK for them?

From whom did you learn that it was your job to make it OK for others?

What does your heart want to say to you right now?

Writing this song and ending my relationship with Crazy Makers was the next big piece of my journey home.

Leaving and getting clear didn't happen easily though.

It took time to get through the dense fog I was in.

I was so confused.

I had accepted that I must be the whole problem if they said I was.

I just kept working on my "patterns" and believed whatever they would say.

Until one day I realized that everything couldn't be my fault and I stopped making it OK for them and began to ask myself what would work for me.

Exploration #8
The belief that self-love is about getting it right

I had lived my whole life striving to get it right. Therefore, I was a perfect mate for a Crazy Maker.

They could point out anything they wanted to blame me for and I'd easily say:

> "Yes, you're right I shouldn't have.
>
> Oh yes, that's just like my mother, I'll fix that.
>
> It's my fault, you can't listen to me."

Being a coach/teacher also was a win/win, as I would happily look to see the validity in all complaints. Surely there was some kernel of truth in it.

I didn't have a framework/definition of what a Crazy Maker was, but when the fog cleared, I had to face the fact that I felt right at home with and had become accustomed to having Crazy Makers around me most of my life. It felt "normal" to me, as it was so familiar.

In time, I gained reality checks and set sail from other crazy islands!

THE BODY DOESN'T LIE

Our heads sure can, but the body can't. Our heads can make up all kinds of stories and rational lies about all kinds of things. However, the body is our truth teller. It will let you know if you listen and pay attention.

When you leave someone/something and you feel relieved, your body is telling you the truth of how you feel.

If you don't miss them, that tells you all you need to know.

List some crazy makers you've left and note if you felt relieved:

I found that after many years of containing my confusion and living with this craziness, when my partner would create chaos and conflict, they would get ice cold and unemotional and I would end up in a fit of anger that was "unexplainable" as if I was feeling what they wouldn't own in themselves.

After I woke up from my coma and sleep state I could see what was happening and was no longer hijacked into those dramas. But it took me a while to unravel. And as the song lyrics indicate:

> *I wish I had put a video recorder up years before, so I could "prove" the crazy making long before I finally believed my own experience and not what they kept saying happened.*

I think one of the greatest crimes committed in crazy-making relationships is that **you end up not trusting yourself**.

You begin to doubt that you heard what you heard, or that they did what you saw them do. You can actually begin to think that you are going crazy.

Your experience becomes invalid.
You can no longer trust what you know
and what your reality is.
You then doubt who you truly are.

I remember going to do more work on myself and while I was there, my beloved coach saw my diligence and she questioned me, "Why are you working on that? You don't have a problem with intimacy."

I told her, "Because my partner said I did." She pointed out to me the reality of who I truly am. She validated that she has experienced me as one of the most open and intimate people she has ever known. She reviewed my other "work" and once again, pointed out the reality. She acknowledged that I have worked on myself for over a decade now.

Then she asked me the question I will forever be grateful for:

"What if
YOU ARE
NOT
The problem?"

When she said it, I was stunned. She said, "I want you to reflect upon this and stop working for now." Moments later I began to thaw from the shock and began to weep, and I noticed some serious relief within my body.

That night, I slept deeply and woke with this clear image:

I was running around holding up a mirror and working very hard to reflect back only their goodness and telling them how wonderful they were while over the mirror came their unclaimed negative aspects, which, I was to retain within myself as me, so they didn't have to face their own "shadow" or negativities.

The agreement was clear: I am to reflect to you how wonderful you are.

And "recycle" and transform all that you dislike in yourself as me.

Another bad fairy tale image! (ugh)

Mirror Mirror on the wall.

What if I am not the problem?

Captive in a prison made of hidden walls

How did I get here?

Why does no one hear my calls?

This makes no sense to me

The confusion blinds

I cannot see

Is this illusion or fantasy?

Is there something wrong with me?

A journal entry from my journey

When I returned home from that weekend workshop I began the journey of testing reality with people who had known me outside my relationship.

It didn't take long to get the universe's validation that I had taken on whatever the Crazy Maker had said and made it my truth.

JUST BECAUSE THEY SAY IT DOES NOT MAKE IT TRUE

I had lost my ability to trust what I was experiencing.

And… I had come to believe what others had told me all my life.

I had become a tapestry that was woven into an asymmetrical shape. There were things that needed to be unwoven and removed.

<u>UNWOVEN</u>

As I *pull* on one thread of truth
I begin the unraveling of an entire lifetime
Of illusions, hypocrisy and lies
Lying to myself
Being lied to
My experience was never validated
I was not seen or heard
As I awaken day-by-day
I'm awestruck at the power of denial

A journal entry from my journey…

Someone recently told me this:

→ *"What others have to say about you says more about them."*

This got me thinking about the messages I was told about who I was as a child and by the Crazy Makers in my life over the years.

I decided to start by exploring these more fully:

What others say about who I am

What I know to be true about who I am

Positive things others have said about who I am:

<u>Negative things others have said about who I am:</u>

Reflect on the list of negative things others have said about you.

Notice if what they said is more about that person and less about you.

For instance, when I was a child, my mom used to say that I was so impatient.

One day recently, my son said to me, "Mom, you're so patient." I flashed inside and thought…Oh, what she said was more about her.

This exercise became quite interesting as I found myself realizing that I had taken what others had said and made it WHO I WAS.

What other things have your parents said about you that aren't true?

<u>What do I know to be true about who I am?</u>

*For many inner travelers **knowing what you know** may have been invalidated and so you may have developed a pattern of forgetting what you know, or denying or waiting for clarity outside yourself to confirm what you know inside.*

Take note if you were not allowed to know what you know.

Further Reflections:

<u>What parts of myself have I lost sight of in the fog of crazy-making relationships?</u>

<u>In what ways have I lost my ability to trust what I am experiencing?</u>

What would be possible if I stopped doubting myself?

<u>Ask your heart what gifts/talents/traits and ways of being you have disowned in yourself because they were invalidated or may even have been criticized.</u>

Notice if you have resistance in naming all your gifts (fear of being boastful—it's not okay to brag or own all that you are, not okay to shine)

If you were a sensitive child emotionally and you were criticized for it, you may have learned to hide your feelings or pretend that you aren't affected as deeply as you truly are.

It is self-loving to claim who you truly are.

This exploration to discover any parts of ourselves that we may have hidden away can be quite fascinating.

A new area of research in the healing arena is how the body shapes itself around its experiences.

I learned in Somatic Healing bodywork, that we take on the shape of our patterns, messages and experiences.

Somatics is derived from the word soma, which means body.

I could see what they were talking about, especially with victims of abuse and physical violence, how the body could cave in the chest, or puff out the chest, or tilt the head from having been slapped so much.

What I couldn't know at this point of my healing journey is what shape I would become after healing more of my childhood traumas and becoming whole.

As I started to reclaim my reality of what was true about me, so many things were going to be changed.

But the journey is not even half over….

Here is a journal entry from where I was on the journey at this point:

I've given myself some time to let things settle
My body is overwhelmed by the input
I can't take in anything else
I've reached critical mass and it feels exhausting
and overwhelming.
In the past two years I've had to digest and integrate
So many truths---
Swallowing years of knowing and pain
Seeking the truth that I already knew again
Can we stop the battle and let things go?
An accounting is done and we are validated
Blending with the body's truth, I can let go
I am not confused much anymore
At least I'm reacting more and not shut down
Or numb and unavailable to myself

Having moved into an open space away from the crazy making, I began to rest and give myself time to recalibrate my "inner guidance system".

I was able to start reclaiming not only the truth of who I was, but also the dreams I had deep in my soul.

From that "open and free" space of my heart, I began to wonder and dream about what was possible.

I began to remember more and more of WHO I REALLY WAS.

I had always had deep longings, questions and dreams to be explored, and I didn't know what was to come.

I didn't realize it at the time, but I was weaving myself back together.
With each untruth I tore out, I replaced it with the truth of who I was.

Not just emotionally, intellectually and spiritually, but physically too.

In this season of my journey, I was starting to notice that I was feeling quite differently within my physical body.

I remember being shocked when I saw a new photo that was taken and couldn't believe that the woman in the picture was me embodied in that shape. I also had let my hair color go natural and let it grow out.

What was true for me was that my body had taken on a shape to not only get love and validation as I mirrored for others WHO THEY SAID I WAS, but also to navigate life from the traumas and experiences I had been through.

With the healing I had done over the years, I had laid the foundation to become more authentically the body shape that represents my true self. However, becoming a mother was a very big step to becoming more authentically embodied as me.

I always wanted to be a mother, and when I became a mother:

My body could shape itself
to reflect my joy, fulfillment,
femininity and the peace within.

My body had shaped itself for years around grief, loss, emptiness, loneliness in my relationship, workaholism, and being who my partner wanted me to be. (I had suffered eight miscarriages and two tubal pregnancies.)

My body was not able to shape itself as an authentic, whole, natural, happy, woman, before this. I had even dyed my hair blonde and cut it short to meet my partner's wishes for two decades.

It is the power of being who I am and living out my dreams that brings my body into full expression. So now my body started taking on a new shape that mirrored my joy!

I am a mothering woman. I love to nurture. I'm a Cancer sign/Leo rising, ENFP Myers Briggs. I'm a musician, artist, dancer, author, coach, speaker. That's me.

<u>What shape has your body taken on that represents the childhood beliefs, adaptations, traumas or "shoulds" of how you look, feel, express yourself?</u>

<u>What did your parents teach you about how your body "should" look?</u>

When you discover the gift of YOUR SELF-LOVE and SELF-COMPASSION, your physical body may change its shape.

Or you may just dress your body to mirror your insides and that will cause you to look and feel quite differently!

I thought the journey would slow down, having fulfilled one of my greatest dreams to become a mother…

However, I think the taste of the good life and happiness propelled me into a new realization…

It's OK to expect and want more!

Exploration #9
The belief that self-love is not expecting too much

As I fulfilled one of my greatest dreams in becoming a mother, I found myself discovering that I had many other dreams within me that I hadn't dared to speak of or act on. One of them was to become an Author. It's like someone turned on the master switch inside of me that said:

What else do I dream of?

What dreams have I discounted as impossible because of my resources?

I had given up having a child after having 8 miscarriages. But my heart kept my dream alive and kept calling out to me when the time was right. Sometimes we have to get really quiet to get clear about our dreams/desires and to connect with what is still possible. I had allowed the grief and sadness to carry me away from my dream.

"If happy little blue birds fly
beyond the rainbow
Why? oh Why? can't I?"

Over The Rainbow

Somewhere over the rainbow, way up high
There's a land that I heard of once
Once in a lullaby

Somewhere over the rainbow, skies are blue
And the dreams that you dared to dream
Really do come true

Someday I'll wish upon a star
And wake up where the clouds are far behind me
Where troubles melt like lemon drops
Away above the chimney tops
That's where you'll find me

Somewhere over the rainbow, skies are blue
And the dreams that you dared to dream
Really do come true

If happy little blue birds fly
Beyond the rainbow
Why oh, why
Can't I?

Lyrics and Music by: E.Y. Harburg and Harold Arlen

<u>Self-loving practice #4</u>
Take time to meditate and listen to yourself

<u>*Travel Guide Tip:*</u>

You do NOT *have to sit still to meditate*

You can walk, dance, bathe, shower, run, yoga, write, journal, sing, or play. Each of us has our own unique ways of connecting to ourselves.

The more I listened to myself, the easier it became. I found these tips to be most helpful:

- **<u>I have to want to hear what I have to say/feel/want</u>**

- **It helps if I follow through on what I hear I want**

    Remember the "my heart wants to song write" message.

- **I may hear, feel and/or see messages**

    Trust my sensations, follow the urges I have, notice the signs

    Allow angels to appear and guides to lead me at times

Meditation allows a new possibility that has not been previously known….

I heard someone say that:

Meditation is not about getting quiet, it's about sorting out which thoughts are yours and which ones are not.

Wow…. That caught my attention… I could use some clarity about which thoughts are mine!

Allowing yourself to be quiet and listen within to what you might dream about or want to experience in your lifetime is a gift.

Take time now on the journey to be still and allow yourself to breathe.

One day while meditating and writing in my journal, I wrote:

<u>Woven By Light</u>

I chose a body suit called GIRL
I was infused with my birthright to BE ME
To express all my gifts
To be courageous, creative,
Playful, kind, generous
Fun, loving
Filled with light
My own unique lovingness
The Weaver wove me
With all I will ever need within me

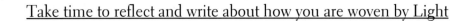

<u>Take time to reflect and write about how you are woven by Light</u>

Some say we all have colors of our aura and light, which makes me think about the rainbow. Everywhere we go, there are people who are making rainbows as they shine their unique light that was woven into them.

Imagining there was gold at the end of that rainbow…and hoping and wishing that I would find that pot of gold, I kept searching.

I had not quite fully owned that the gold and treasure I was seeking was all woven within me.

It's like having the words/knowledge and information, but not integrating it into your emotions and body.

I had to retrace some steps, it seemed.

I needed to explore some other territories in order to find my way back home

I was in complete denial about my patterns of giving myself away and tolerating being used.

Remember the not so pretty prince charming song *"Let My Guard Down"* on page 54 about being used and fooled?

Well, I had skimmed over that in a very short page or two…

Not surprisingly I guess, I wasn't quite ready to deal with that pattern in my life.

So, one sunny day I'm sitting in my naturopathic doctor's office telling him about this sensation I was having and difficulty with feeling like "I can't be myself in my relationship, they don't see me for who I truly am."

He listened and then kept asking me, "So do you give yourself away?"

I said, "No, that's not it."

He said, "It sounds like you're giving yourself away."

I said, "No."

This went on for several minutes and he let me rationalize and talk as good talkers can do…until the final time he asked me, and I could finally hear it and the tears burst out of my eyes like rockets in red glare.

He hit the bull's eye.

OK reader, so you may have been able to glean through my writing so far that I absolutely have given myself away. However, words do not indicate a person's level of understanding and ability to take action upon something.

I had written a song about it, lived it out for most of my life and was just now able/ready/willing/needing to:
DEAL WITH IT. ACCEPT IT. HEAL.

Why would I give myself away?
Why would I tolerate being used by someone?

These were the right questions to take me where I needed to go.

What I didn't know
was that the answer
to these questions
was going to require
inner resources and resilience
that I didn't know
existed within myself at that time.

I was about to embark on a journey that I could not have imagined.

IT'S NOT OKAY

Did you just expect that we would somehow forget?
And one day this would not really have an affect?

How could you just stand by and watch the fists fly?
and block out the nights when all we did was cry?

Where were you when it was happening to me?
You say that you didn't know and you didn't see?

How is it possible that you missed the signs?
Of a hurting body and crossed boundary lines

Where was the protection? How you couldn't stop it?
Upon further reflection, how you wouldn't stop?

And you still don't seem to understand
What it's like living in confusion land

My head said yes, but you said no
But somewhere inside I knew it was so

118

I kept asking and you kept lying
And that's how we learn to keep denying
That it ever happened at all
Put on a happy face and play ball

Inside the truth sleeps until one day
Light shines in the dark places hidden away
And we remember the horror and a face
That took our innocence without a trace

Used our body and twisted our mind
To believe that we were at fault
Or one of a very special kind

The trail of victims is long and deep
And the pain won't end
until some die in their sleep

Why aren't children protected in their homes?
Why do victims end up feeling so alone?

I dare to speak out and pray my friend
That this crime against so many, will come to an end.

It's NOT Okay to abuse and use anyone
It's NOT Okay to abuse
It's NOT Okay

Lyrics Written By: Linda Newlin © 2011

It's Not Okay to abuse and use anyone, especially ourselves.

As I wrote these words to this song it occurred to me that there are so many forms that abuse can take. What was becoming quite clear to me is that I had such comfort with "being used."

I won't describe the whole healing journey that I traveled through this landscape, because it is a whole other book. However, I would love to share the key guideposts that served me in finding my inner knowing.

It is my hope that if you have been "used or abused" (emotionally, physically, or sexually) that you find your way to the LIGHT OF TRUTH and HEALING so that you can be free to have healthy, peaceful and passionate loving relationships that nurture and bring safety to your world.

What is important is to find answers to why you do what you do today.

As I tell my clients, it is not important that you remember all the details of the events to find truth. If you sense that you were abused, then go with that.

I had a male client tell me that he had night terrors sometimes and that he was sleeping with a bat by his bed and wasn't feeling safe at night now that his dog had recently died. I said, "Were you abused as a child?" He said, "Yes my dad used to come in at night." Even though he had known he was abused in the past, he didn't make the connection to his current stresses as possible residual abuse trauma that could be healed.

The self-loving thing to do is to heal yourself.

<u>Self-loving practice #5</u>
Heal thyself

We heal so we can live free and claim our wholeness.

Let me start with the most important truth:

YOU ARE MUCH BIGGER THAN ANYTHING

THAT HAS EVER HAPPENED TO YOU...

Remember you were woven by Light...

What I did remember after writing the song, "It's Not Okay" is that for more than twenty years, I had been asking my family if something had happened.

The answer was always no.

But as the words to this song so accurately describe,

But somewhere inside I knew

I could feel a different healing sensation when the truth was finally validated. Yes, I had been abused as a child and young adult. I was used as a sexual object while I slept at night. This uncovering of the secret helped me to understand why I had doubted my inner guidance and my knowing for years. It also explained my choices in relationship partners.

When somewhere inside you know…but you're told "no, you're wrong," you learn to doubt yourself.

It was such a relief to finally know that what I thought happened really did happen. And I could settle into my intuition in a whole new way. This validation helped to explain the patterns of behavior that had played out in my adult life as:

People who love me "use me"

Giving myself away

(financially, emotionally, physically)

When I coach clients today whose journey has included forms of abuse (either physical, sexual, emotional or financial), I emphasize that it's not important that you remember every detail or even who was abusing you.

For your growth and healing, you can work with the manifestations of how you are in your life. The probability of the abuse helps to validate and make sense of the confusion and answers the questions:

Why do I shut down around angry people?

Why do I keep attracting people like this?

Why am I depressed, disconnected from my body/can't feel?

Why do I over-protect/under-protect my children?

Why do I allow others to mistreat me?

Why do I tolerate abuse from others?

Why am I hyper-vigilant?

Why do I feel safe only when I'm alone? Or why don't I feel safe alone?

Why do I live "outside" my body and numb out?

Why am I addicted to substances/behaviors?

Why do I suppress my feelings?

Why do I not like sex?

Why do I feel shame about liking sex?

Why do I not protect myself?

Why do I say yes when I want to say no?

Why do I have trouble setting boundaries?

My passion for helping people heal from past abuse is based in my own experience and it is my desire to have all survivors heal and find their path to freedom and safety so they can truly love themselves and others in their life who are also healthy and whole. I envision a world of people thriving not surviving.

A portion of the profits of the CD and book sales will be given to organizations that are working to end all forms of abuse.

For me, I realized that the worst manifestation of being abused is that we might create an equation within ourselves of:

LOVE = ABUSE

This belief and familiar pattern can run throughout our lives until we heal and transform it with what our heart knows to be true.

<u>Love is not abuse. Love is not about using someone.</u>

Whether you were abused physically or emotionally, this equation can be operating in some area of your life.

Maybe you abuse yourself…. I surely did.

Workaholic
Perfectionist
Unrealistic expectations
Drove my body to collapse
Couldn't just BE (had to be doing things)
Negative self-talk/internal critic

Staying in unhealthy relationships
Sugar - eating foods I was allergic to
Pretending
Going along with things I didn't want to
Saying Yes when I wanted to say No
Believing crazy makers

Those are just some of the self-abusive behaviors I was engaged in.

Circle the ones that apply to you: *some you may have stopped doing.*
Validate yourself for your growth and progress!

Being self critical

Focusing on the body parts I don't like

Never feeling good enough

Expecting more and more of myself

Not being able to rest and do nothing

Over/under exercising

Beating myself up for not doing something

Comparing myself to others

Isolating

"Shoulding" on myself

Feeling guilty if I'm not doing for others

Not spending money on myself

Sabotaging my health/weight

Addictions (alcohol/smoke/drugs/shop)

Not seeking help to heal

Putting others first always

Making excuses

Not letting myself be happy

Hiding my attractiveness and sensuality

Staying too long

Waiting

Letting others talk me into things

Ignoring my own inner wisdom

Taking all the blame/blaming self

Holding a belief that I am bad/wrong

Believing what others say

Pretending to be happy when I'm not

Lying to myself/being lied to

Tolerating abuse

Giving up on my dreams

Talking myself out of what I want

Doubting myself

Shaming myself/letting others shame me

Staying small

Calling myself names

Denying my own needs

Refusing to accept help/support

Not claiming my gifts and my dreams

Saying yes when I mean no

Talking myself out of what I want

Not taking action

Blaming myself for what happened

<u>Emotional abuse</u> = Parent using you as a spouse/trusted confidant, making you the object of their neediness. Like a parasite and you're the host. "Make me feel good, heal my pain, do what I could never do," living vicariously through you, creating fear and anxieties, hating the opposite sex, blackmailing, "I'll kill myself if you don't," threatening abandonment, teasing, not believing you.

<u>Physical abuse</u> = hitting, beating, burning, slapping, isolating punishment, torture, starving, forcing you to eat, withholding affection, kicking you out.

<u>Sexual abuse</u> = rape, inappropriate touching as children (older child to younger), sodomy, elder to child/teen, sex with minor, inappropriate "staring at breasts," ogling, objectifying, using teens as "pseudo spouses" or like a girlfriend/boyfriend.

<u>Note any forms of abuse that you endured as a child/adult</u>:

As children when any of the above happens to us, we are linking it with LOVE.

Some May Blame Themselves

How could this be possible?
How does that happen?

It does not make logical sense.

When there is no information we fill in the vacuum.

Someone is abused.
The abuser does not acknowledge it happened.
The victim confronts the abuser and they deny it.

The victim has to reconcile:

> *Is my experience real or did I make it up?*
> *Maybe I was wrong*
> *Maybe I dreamed it*
> *Do I believe myself or them?*

Sometimes when the abuser is confronted they tell a very different story and the victim is now the "guilty" party who brought the abuse on themselves. This is often the case in rape cases.

Abuse may shut down the inner guidance system

Other times, there is nothing reported as the victim/survivor was told they would be hurt/killed if they did….

Other times, the victim/survivor is made to feel special and therefore won't tell the "little secret" that the perpetrator "loves you" more than the others.

Who is the victim/survivor going to blame?

This truly is the second crime. The first is the action… the second is that no one takes responsibility for violating boundaries or hurting you, so the abused may fill in the blanks with:

I must be bad…
I must have caused this…
I should have…
I could have…
It's my fault…

The shame that can occur with sexual abuse can feed self-blaming.

Another manifestation can be extreme guilt.

If I enjoy this, then I'm bad.
I'm not strong enough to stop this.
I must deserve this somehow.
If only I were…

Sometimes the abuser makes the person feel special:

You're the only one who understands me
I can't talk to anyone but you
Only you care for me in ways no one else does
I couldn't live without you
I love you
You're my favorite
(Altar boy, scout, child, relative, student, athlete, lover)

Sometimes the abuser uses their power over the other: this takes many forms and typically creates the "secrets" we keep. This includes all types of authority: parent, sibling, other relative, religious leader, coach, teacher, trainer, troop leader, mentor, babysitter.

Silence is maintained and the abuser is protected because of his or her authority and sometimes this type of abuser will threaten to hurt their victims if they tell.

The experience of abuse is traumatic and it is a crime.

But the worst thing is that when the abuse is over, the survivor may continue to be "traumatized" in their life by the patterns they play out because of the equations they attach to love.

Some equations that get created:

> *Love is being abused by those who care about me.*
> *Those who abuse me make me feel special.*
> *Those who say they love me hurt me.*
> *Those who should be protecting me, aren't.*

Older adults taking advantage of younger children/teens:

Sometimes a person is taken advantage of and it is not registered as abuse.

In this case, we might see patterns in this person's life of allowing others to take advantage of them.

This person might not find support and long-term commitments in their loving relationships.

They might have patterns around going along with things they don't really want to do, but something seems OK about it and they end up in situations they might not have expected to be in.

This can happen when drugs and alcohol abuse are involved.

The person is not actually present for the abuse so they are not fully registering what is happening.

And in many abuse cases, especially incest or adult to child relationships, LOVE is part of the equation.

So if Love = Abuse

What type of relationships will I continue to attract?

Take note if you have patterns of going along with things you don't really want to do or have ways you have linked LOVE and ABUSE in subtle ways:

How do I treat myself? How did my parents treat themselves?

132

How do I tolerate abuse from others I "love"?

Ask your heart what needs to be healed

Often people start their healing journey with a "wake up"…

For some that's a loss, a divorce, and for some it's a birth of a child.

For some it's the death of the abuser.

For some it's the remembering and exploring of memories and answers to the internal "gut feelings" that something bad happened.

For others, it's questions about why they feel/think in certain ways and are finding the connections to formative sexual experiences that shaped them.

Please remember and note:
    People are not born to seek out abusive situations.

    A child does not know love to be anything other than positive, nurturing, protective and constant until the child experiences some break in that reality.

    People are not born to feel shame about themselves or doubt their experience as real.

Why take this journey of healing?

    Because you deserve to know the truth so you can bring your internal guidance system back on line. You will find more of yourself when you release the feelings that keep you from being free. You deserve to sleep in peace at night and not fear who or what might be coming into your room. You deserve to have mutually loving and giving relationships that fulfill your needs and honor your boundaries.

Because you deserve to know that what you sense happened within you is true. You deserve to reclaim your safe space in this world and release the trauma from your body and emotions so you can live a fulfilling sexual/sensual life and have deep intimate connections with those you love.

> For some the healing journey frees the addictions they've been using to numb out from all the past hurt and suffering experienced.

> For some it's finding safe connections with others who are capable of really being present, loving and nurturing.

People who are abused learn NOT to trust their own experience and instincts. Their guidance system is taken off line.

They have an inner knowing that this behavior and abuse is NOT okay; however, the abuser keeps telling them that it is *(in words or in repeated actions)*

How would a child know that what is happening to them isn't normal?

Each of us will define whatever we received in childhood as love and normal.

It's not until many people reach mid life that they rediscover the truth within and unravel the confusion and strange equations they have formulated to deal with the reality they experienced.

Sometimes it's not until the person meets someone else who shares an experience that they begin to question whether it was "right" or really did happen.

For some, it's in a book or a song.

<u>What I know/sense that happened to me in my childhood that wasn't OK</u>

<u>What will be possible for me if I heal?</u>

136

If I Had My Way....
Children Would Be Cherished

If I Had My Way

Long ago and far away
Before the world had come to this
I took for granted how my life would be
Assuming that my freedom
Would be free

Before these evening shadows fell
I reveled in the light of day
I rarely ever cried
My patience wasn't tried
And heroes never died

But if I had my way
Things would be different
Danger wouldn't come
From a sky of blue
Choices would be clear
Strangers would be kinder
Love a little blinder
As it saved the day
If I had my way

Every now and then it seems
We live our lives to such extremes
Racing all around never homeward bound
Losing what we found

But if I had my way
Things would be different
No one would believe
That a lie was true

Choices would be clear
Wisdom would be heeded
Warnings never needed
This is what I'd pray
If I had my way

The milk of human kindness
Would seek us out and find us
And color all the words we say

And hearts would come alive
Instead of breaking
No one would believe
That a lie was true
Angels would appear
Children would be cherished
Hope would never perish
Faith would not betray

If I had my way

Lyrics and Music By: Jack Murphy & Frank Wildhorn

If I had my way…

This song was so powerful for my healing process because it mirrored the "waking up" that I was doing shortly after my son was born and my abuse was being addressed.

These words represent the vision and hope/dream I have for the world.

I have always wanted hope to thrive and for our world to be different.

I knew deep down inside myself that what I had experienced as "love" was not all there was. Love was not abuse, the world is not dangerous, children could be cherished and protected.

AND my heart assured me that love was the answer.

What creates more love? What do we need?

Humans have two basic needs

Safety and Connection

Somatic expert and trainer Staci Haines helps survivors of abuse to heal through trauma release and re-education of the body. She described to me the reality that:

We cannot connect with another person unless we feel safe.

This then must mean that:

If I want to be more connected to myself…

I have to create safety for myself.

Thus began my journey to ask the all-important next question….

How do I make it safe for me?

I went back to my list of ways I was abusing myself and realized that it was not safe to live inside my "embodied" self with all of that going on. What was operating inside me was:

Fear of punishment, ridicule, rejection, intolerance, unrealistic expectations, perfectionism, fear of failure, lack of forgiveness, limited compassion/empathy, non-acceptance, holding it all together, suppressing feelings, proving, people pleasing.

That all sounds abusive, doesn't it?

It wasn't until I could shift the internal environment within myself to a safe haven that I could begin to connect with myself more deeply.

I could then hear that still, small voice within me. The clarity of the messages and connection were transformative and amazing.

The work became about keeping myself safe so I could stay connected with my body, mind, emotions and spirit.

Once I became connected, I could feel my feelings and begin to heal even more deeply.

141

Music is one of the most powerful healing tools I have found.

Resilience is what heals us. Some other resilience tools/activities: art, nature, animals and creativity.

Staci Haines is co-founder of Gen Five, a non-profit 501(c)(3) whose mission is to end abuse in five generations. Knowing the magnitude and breadth of abuse in the world, she has a realistic vision and goal. She tirelessly works to heal individuals and collective communities around sexual trauma and issues related to survivors healing their sexuality.

If she had her way, sexual abuse would no longer exist by the year 2350. A vision and mission worthy of our support.

Now take some time to reflect on what your vision and mission would be.

<u>If I had my way, how would the world be different?</u>

<u>What do I care about?</u>

<u>Who do I care about?</u>

For me, I care about changing the world. I always have. It is who I am.

I traveled in Up With People in 1982 and it was our vision to change the world through music and community service. As I write this book and listen to the words in the CD of *Love Your Self*, I realize that I am carrying on that worthy mission. I am an idealist.

I believe that the world does change, one person at a time. I also believe now that self-love is the most effective change tool we have right now.

And it seems to me that:

Self-love is one of the answers to creating a peaceful world

If someone loves themselves, they won't abuse others or themselves.

If someone loves themselves, they will create safety and they will connect.

If someone loves themselves, they will claim their gifts and share.

If someone loves themselves, they will love others unconditionally.

The Beatles said it and it's true:

All you need is love

They just didn't have room in the melody line to say

All you need is self-love

<u>Right now on the journey what is the most self-loving thing I can do for myself?</u>

Be kind to yourself...
Alleviate your suffering...
Be Who you Are...
Want what you want

In this next song I wrote the words to myself as a reminder to create safety and stop being in abusive relationships.

As you will see I credit Delilah, the national radio show host, in the lyrics, as I believe she has inspired healing in millions of people over the years. When I was suffering miscarriages or broken relationships, I would just happen upon her show and always hear the exact words I needed to hear from her...and the songs she played brought healing to my hurting heart.

So, my deepest gratitude to you, Delilah!

You change the world with your gifts and generous heart that exudes love and compassion every night you reach out over the radio waves to listeners.

Thank you for being who you are and giving inspiration to others to heal and move on!

There will always be more!

Song to Self

If I don't remember the pain
I will tolerate insane
If I don't say ouch
That really hurts
Don't do it again
But I think it
And I don't say it

Stand up and Walk out
Even in the rain
No more excuses
No more lies and pain
There is no honor here
Tear after unhappy tear
Move out and Move on
Another lifetime, Come and Gone

Listen to Delilah's song
Sing I will survive
Cry all night long
Then turn and face the rising dawn
And remember the pain
So you never, go back again.

Oh remember the pain, so you never
Never, ever go back again.

Lyrics By: Linda Newlin ©2011

What excuses am I currently using in my life?

What lies do I tell myself and/or others?

It takes courage, curiosity and compassion to answer these two questions.

These patterns of **making excuses and lying** can block our freedom and our path to living the life we dream of and have always wanted.

After looking at my lies and excuses:

I discovered that I had a pattern of forgetting.

I was programmed to remember only the good stuff.

I was programmed to take the crumbs I received and make them into a feast.

I was good at pretending and lying to myself.

I told myself I was happy when I wasn't.

I forgot my unhappiness.

I didn't even register the pain.

I blocked out the tears, the frustrations, the walking on eggshells, the frantic repair moves.

I learned to blame myself for everything that wasn't working.

I was always wrong.

It was as if I forgot what really happened.

My heart cried out, "**YES, THAT'S IT.**"

I had learned that I should forgive and forget.

But the lyrics said, "I must remember"

Many of us learned that we have to forgive and turn the other cheek, so this new perspective on forgiveness was quite radical and I sensed that this was going to change my life.

FORGIVE AND REMEMBER

My heart assured me that forgiving is not about forgetting.

When we forgive someone we are not supposed to forget what they did.

If we do, we can potentially stay in abusive/unsafe situations.

If we forgive and remember, we can keep ourselves safe from repeat abuses. And we can free ourselves to be whole and more at peace.

Why should I forgive?

Not to let the other person off the hook who has hurt me… but to free myself.

When I forgive, I get to stop living in the past and being stuck with the "holding" energy it takes to hold grudges and pain of the past hurts.

And what do I get when I forgive myself and others?

Freedom to live in the PRESENT

"I will remember that I did the best I could...
and love heals all things just like it should."

I Forgive Myself

I forgive myself for lying about what I see
I forgive myself for denying what was real for me
I forgive myself for hiding the truth all the time
I forgive myself for staying far too long in line

But I won't forget
I must remember
That those who hurt me
Aren't safe to render
A place to be free
No more surrender

I forgive myself for losing my fortune and my voice
I forgive myself for blaming myself for my choice
I forgive myself for letting courage slip away
I forgive myself for trusting the words they would say

I will remember that I did the best I could
And love heals all things just like it should

I will remember that I did the best I could
And love heals all things just like it should

And love heals all…just like it should

Lyrics by: Linda Newlin © 2012

153

Forgive and Remember

Think of a grudge/pain or hurt you carry with you:

Who is the person and what did they do/or didn't do that hurt you?

How long have you been carrying it?

What would be possible if you could let this go and forgive this person?

Is there someone in your life who is holding a grudge against you?

For what and for how long have they held it against you?

What would be possible if you could forgive yourself for this and let it go?

Self-loving practice #6
Forgive myself and others

<u>What resistance am I aware of that gets in the way of me forgiving myself or others?</u>

<u>Ask your heart, what can I do to release this resistance?</u>

Holding on to the past is a form of vindictiveness and it can destroy us over time. In William Blake's poem "The Poison Tree" he describes how "our wrath doth grow." When we are holding on to the past it's almost as if we are saying:

"I will keep drinking the poison hoping you will die."

Vindictiveness blocks our connection to our heart and our freedom to live in the present

The power of releasing the poison that is inside us is hard to describe. By letting go of the past we make more space within and can discover more of our true self.

<u>Reflect on how you have been vindictive to yourself and others.</u>

Self-loving practice #7
Release vindictiveness

And then my heart told me that …

> **I had the power to stop suffering and to release the past so I could become fully present to my life.**

No more holding grudges, no more pretending.

<u>What else have I been holding on to that needs to be released, so I can live healthy and free?</u>

It is self-loving to forgive and release our vindictiveness.

Is anything unforgiveable? (I say no… but I have many clients who say yes).

"It's unforgiveable that I had an abortion".

"I made my partner have an abortion."

When I work with men and women who have had abortions in their past, many struggle to forgive themselves as they believe that it is not forgivable.

I always then ask…

Do you want to be forgiven? (if you say yes)

I invite you into this healing forgiveness visualization:

Be in a quiet space.

Breathe into your heart and become present.

If you have a guardian angel/spirit guide or belief in higher power, you can invite them in to be with you during this visualization.

Feel yourself surrounded by white light (like a ray of sunshine surrounding you).

Imagine the spirit/soul of the aborted baby's spirit coming to greet you. This spirit has something important to tell you.

Be curious and open to what you hear/sense or feel.

From this connected space, you may ask any questions.

Tell this baby spirit anything you need/want to say.

Honor the reasons why you made that choice at the time.

Say whatever you want to say and if it feels right, ask this spirit to forgive you.

And then forgive yourself here in the light…

Allow yourself to feel the freedom and grace of being forgiven.

If you have had multiple abortions, you may repeat with each spirit if you wish

You can also use this type of visualization with people who are deceased and with whom you have something to clear or heal.

You can use it with a perpetrator if you were abused. You might have loved someone who has killed himself and you didn't get to say goodbye.

Allow yourself to experience whatever happens as you express your intention to be free of past hurts and let the poison out so you can live freely and have more space for your love and wholeness to emerge.

Your heart will lead you through this.

If it's true we learn negative love and can act from our patterns unconsciously, then we make choices that aren't from WHO WE ARE and we hurt ourselves and others on our path.

Do you want to be forgiven for the ways you have acted unconsciously and hurt others?

When we ask for forgiveness, we free ourselves and the other person from the chains of the past hurts, grudges and pain that rob us of the present.

<u>Ask your heart what you need to forgive yourself for</u>.

Forgiveness is not about making something right;
It is about healing the past and accepting
that we all do the best we can
at each moment of our lives.

In my own journey of learning to forgive it was easier for me to forgive those who had hurt me, because I could *forgive and remember* and that meant I could protect myself from those who weren't safe. I could let go of the hurt, but I didn't put myself in harm's way again. Forgiving them didn't mean I had to spend time with them.

The freedom we gain from releasing the past is worth forgiving.

Forgiveness is about giving ourselves
the gift of freedom and space
to be authentically who we were meant to be.

And then there is **APOLOGY…**

Does the other person have to say they're sorry for me to move on?

What do you want/expect from people who hurt you?

I was coaching a client and she was saying how she wished she would get an apology letter from her ex-husband. We discussed it and then I said,

> **"Why don't you write it for him?"**

She said, "What a great idea. I'll write myself the apology I deserve."

She went off that week and wrote what she wanted him to have written to her, and afterwards she was feeling empowered and free.

So empowered that she decided to write ALL the apology letters she should have received throughout her lifetime.

It has now become a book that will be released in 2013 called:

Sorry So Sorry, Apology letters I should have received, but never will

By: Mary Boone Wellington

I invite you to experience the gift of writing your much awaited apology letter(s):

Write the letters you've been waiting and hoping for that will likely never come.

Let yourself experience whatever arises as you "give to yourself" what you have wanted and needed.

Self-loving practice #8
Apologize and allow others to apologize

Now that you've experienced the power of receiving the apology(s) you have been wanting, let yourself take action to apologize to those you have hurt and lift the burden of any shame or guilt that you have kept inside.

<u>List all the people you would like to apologize to and ask forgiveness from:</u>

Note how and when you will apologize and ask for forgiveness from these people, so you can be free and find peace.

If the person is deceased, you can write the letter and release/keep it. Or do it verbally in a visualization format. Whatever works for you with this person.

When we take responsibility for our actions and repair with those we have hurt, more space is created for love and possibility.

Love heals all things, just like it should.

How do I come home to me?

*Not out saving
    the next one I see?*

TIME TO GO HOME (and love me too)

How do I come home to me?
Not out saving the next one I see
Somewhere inside I know what I know
How crazy it is to never stay home
But where am I? and where do I live?
Out there with lovers I lived to give to
How do I reclaim, and choose what's sane?
Me, myself and my good name

Giving myself away, don't know how to stay
Loving myself within and not just loving him
Crazy Yes, Crazy No
It's back home that I must go
Claim the love and light that's mine
Gather the parts I left behind
Wake up and name all that is true
Its time to go home and love me too

Don't need a man to tell me
Who I am and what they want to see
Won't color or cut off my wavy hair
Won't wear the clothes they want me wear, No

Momma's crazy way was this
But a sad lonely prison I'll never miss
I'm over making it OK for you
Breaking free is what I will do
Wake up and name all that is true
It's time to go home and love me too.
It's time to go home

Lyrics Written By: Linda Newlin © 2011

What does it mean to come home to me and love me too?

Here are some things self-love and self-compassion can bring to you:

- Claim the gifts I was given and use them in my life/family/world
- Nurture my body (massage, exercise, healthy foods, sexual pleasure)
- Learn new things
- Live my dreams
- Buy what I truly want/Live how I truly want
- Fulfill my own needs/Ask for my needs to be met
- Validate myself and my experience as real
- Heal my childhood so I can live free in the present
- Forgive myself and others
- Give up addictions/addictive behaviors
- Let go of the past
- Trust myself
- Ask for what I want/Believe I can have what I want
- Express my sensuality/sexuality fully
- Leave abusive relationships/friendships/family dynamics
- Find clarity in confusing situations
- Grieve losses and heal past hurts
- Release trauma from the body with somatics healing
- Be courageous and bold (try new things)
- Share with others my experience and gifts
- Honor my truth that I AM a unique Spirit having a human experience
- Express myself fully and authentically
- Create a supportive circle of friends/community
- Cherish my uniqueness/Be the treasure that I am
- Listen to my heart
- Look for the answers within
- Seek support when necessary
- Release repressed feelings that keep me from feeling alive and joyful!

<u>This has been my journey back home to myself…</u>

> To stop making it OK for others
>
> To break free of the patterns that had been inhibiting my authenticity and forward motion
>
> To wake up and name all that is true
>
> To find my way home to myself
>
> To learn to love myself fully
>
> To feel what I actually felt

In order to be at home with myself, I needed to feel my feelings.

Our Feelings Orient Us

And yet as children we aren't allowed to feel all our feelings–no wonder we have difficulty knowing where we are and being oriented along our journeys…

<u>What feelings were allowed to be expressed in my family?</u>

<u>What feelings were NOT allowed to be expressed by me in my family?</u>

If we don't feel and express our feelings, we can find ourselves reacting with historical emotions that have been kept trapped and locked away within us in very sporadic volcanic eruptions.

<u>Reflect on how you may have learned to "stuff" your emotions in childhood.</u>

172

When a child has a tantrum you can see that immediately following the release of the emotions and physical stress they are clear and present and cooperative.

We feel better after a good cry.

Or some feel "freer" after getting things off our chest and saying what they've been suppressing.

<u>How might my life change if I could express emotions in a healthy way?</u>

Emotions are Energy

Emovare – "to move"

If we feel our emotions, they can move.

<u>If we do not feel our feelings:</u>

We lose our sense of direction

We contract and stay small

We lose life force energy

We doubt our reality

We suppress and get depressed

We implode/create illness/disease/die

We can rage (due to historic anger releases)

We numb out with addictions to cover our pain

We may stay stuck in unsatisfying relationships

We can't be free to be who we are

Joy is blocked

SELF-LOVE IS...

The nurturing of our whole SELF.

It is the care and feeding of our bodies,
the nourishment of our minds,
the full expression of our feelings,
the cultivation of our gifts within
and the discovery of what brings us joy
at each stage of our life.

What is the most self-loving thing I can do for my emotional self?

What is the most self-loving thing I can do for my body?

Acknowledge what actions I do take to love myself at this point in my life.

What self-loving/self-compassionate things do I wish I were doing for myself that I just can't seem to get around to doing?

What is calling me now that wants to be expressed?

Your heart knows, even if you are not quite clear in this moment.

Listening to My Heart:

Sit quietly and breathe.
Focus on your heart.
Ask your heart what it wants.
Receive the answer(s).
Write down what you
hear/feel/sense.

Repeat often!

<u>Self-loving practice #10</u>
Listen to your heart

<u>What gets in the way of me listening to my heart?</u>

Reflections:

How can I know what I want if I don't inquire within myself?

Will I wait for others to tell me what I want?

Will I wait for signs to guide me?

Where will I end up if I don't make a choice?

What will I miss out on if I don't follow my heart?

What is the pay off for remaining stuck?

<u>Self-loving practice #11</u>
Take action to fulfill your heart's desires

<u>What did my parents teach me about taking action to fulfill my heart's desires?</u>

<u>What story is your head telling you now about having what your heart desires</u>
We can't because…It's too late…We don't have the money now…

<u>What would be possible if you stopped listening to that story?</u>

<u>Self-loving practice #12</u>
Allow yourself to be happy at work and at home

Some people actually have an unconscious belief that it is a crime to be happy. Especially if your parents were unhappy.

<u>What did my parents teach me about being happy at work and at home?</u>

What was your parents' relationship to their work?

How do you relate to your work?

Did you choose your career/or did you follow/reject your parents' footsteps?

When you were a child, what did you dream of doing as your life's work?

Reflect on how your childhood dreams have/have not manifested:

<u>Self-loving practice #13</u>
Validate and acknowledge yourself

<u>**Write your own performance review:**</u> *the one you've always wanted your boss to write to you. Acknowledge who you are to your company, your customers and your colleagues.*

<u>*My Performance Review*</u>:

Notice what it feels like to speak your own truth and validate yourself.

What if I loved me...like I love you?

Would I tell myself positive things?

Would I celebrate my growth and successes?

Would I nurture and invest in my dreams?

Would I let myself experiment and fail without ridicule?

Would I claim my power to create the life I wanted?

Would I encourage and support myself gently?

Would I treat myself like the beloved?

Would I go on a honeymoon (even for one)?

Would I write myself love letters?

Self-loving practice #14
Write love letters to yourself

Write a Love Letter <u>To Yourself</u>! Please use extra pages because this one isn't enough!
*(If it helps, write the letter you have always dreamed **someone else** would write to you and ask your heart what it always wanted to hear.)*

Read your letter out loud and notice what sensations you feel inside yourself. Write those sensations down:

<u>*Read it again*</u>:
Feel the power of your validation.

Write down what you sense in your body as you read it the second time:

Notice if there are things you left out of your love letter that you wish you had included:

WRITE them here:

Notice any resistances coming up to validating and loving yourself through writing appreciation and acknowledgements.

<u>What did I learn about self-validation and treating myself like the beloved?</u>

Other letters you may wish to write:
Remember the power of the apology letters from others to you?

If you are a parent, write a letter to you from your children.

You may wish to write a letter to you from your parents.

These are the letters you have always wanted them to send to you. They say all the things you have longed for them to say to you. *If your parents are deceased you can still write the letters you always wanted them to write to you.*

Read the letters out loud and feel the transforming power of your self-love and validation.

The Woman I AM
is happy I'm here
With nothing to fear
I will shine like a light!

THE WOMAN I AM

The woman I am, says what I mean
Lives my own dream
Dances til dawn

The Woman I am, loves how I feel
Is free and real
Knows what I want

I want to be me, kind, lovin' and bold
I want to play free
Change the world til I'm old
I want to grow, I want to soar
I want all this
And so much more

The Woman I Am
Plays my own part
Gives my whole heart
Embraces the night

The woman I am
Is happy I'm here
With nothing to fear
I will shine like a light, I will shine like a light
I will shine like a light!

Lyrics Written By: Linda Newlin © 2011

<u>Self-loving practice #15</u>
Be who you are and want what you want

These two guiding principles are key to living from your heart
and being self-loving/self-compassionate:

Who am I?

What do I want?

In any given day when you have to decide about anything, you can use these two guiding compasses:

<u>Who am I?</u> This will ground your decisions in your values and what you care about. You will act as your whole present loving self.

<u>What do I want?</u> This will ground your actions to be loving and clear.

For example: You have just had an argument with someone. In order to clear this experience, you connect with who you are and what you want in this situation.

From this connected and authentic place you enter into the conflict resolution with your heart present and your intentions focused on what you want and who you want to be in this interaction.

Staying focused on the outcome you want helps to keep you in the present and open to something new to show up instead of your old programmed patterns you've learned around conflict resolution.

Possibilities expand when we are connected to:

WHO WE ARE and WHAT WE WANT.

The power of visioning and living how we want to live becomes easier when we are present to ourselves and acting from our desired outcomes.

Ask your heart:

<u>Who am I?</u>

<u>What do I want in my life now?</u>

Note: You don't have to know how to make this happen. Learning to trust our heart's messages takes time. I had never written a song before. Once I stopped resisting it took ten minutes to write the first one. And it took ten minutes to write the next one.

I did have time to song write.

It became easier to trust that my heart knew what she was talking about! ☺

I also had an outrageous message from my heart back in 2003 that <u>I was going to have a baby.</u>

After suffering eight miscarriages and two tubal pregnancies, I had every right to think my heart was more than a bit out of touch with reality.

However, my heart kept calling out to me and convinced me that it was possible and to try. It was after all WHO I WAS and WHAT I WANTED.

<u>**Miracles of miracles I had my son at age 40**</u>.

Now you know why I had to write this book. Our hearts know what's right for us.

I am continuing to learn time and again that my heart knows who I am and what I want.

My heart knows the what, the when and the how.

I just need to listen, trust and take action on the things my heart tells me.

The joy of being who I am
and expressing my light in the world!

This Little Light of Mine

This little light of mine I'm gonna let it shine
This little light of mine I'm gonna let it shine
This little light of mine I'm gonna let it shine
Let it shine, let it shine, let it shine

With my heart and soul, I'm gonna let it shine
With my heart and soul, I'm gonna let it shine
With my heart and soul, I'm gonna let it shine
Let it shine, let it shine, let it shine

Everywhere I go, I'm gonna let it shine
Everywhere I go, I'm gonna let it shine
Everywhere I go, I'm gonna let it shine
Let it shine, let it shine, let it shine

Won't let anyone blow it out, I'm gonna let it shine
Won't let anyone blow it out, I'm gonna let it shine
Won't let anyone blow it out, I'm gonna let it shine
Let it shine, let it shine, ALL THE TIME

This little light of mine, I'm gonna let it shine
This little light of mine, I'm gonna let it shine
This little light of mine, I'm gonna let it shine
Let it shine, let it shine, let it shine

Public Domain Traditional Song (words modified)

<u>Self-loving practice #16</u>
Do what you love and shine your light

Exercise: Close your eyes and breathe. Bring to mind something that you have loved doing. See yourself and feel yourself doing it. Notice the sensations in your body as you engage in this. Notice the flow within you. How does it feel to be doing what you love?

<u>Write down the sensations:</u>

Sometimes the thing that lights us up is something from childhood that we haven't allowed ourselves to do in our recent life. You can try this experience with other things you love doing. Notice what it is that lights you up about this.

Take time to write about all the things that light you up:

<u>What Lights Me Up Is</u>

Sometimes we can excuse what lights us up as "not something I can do to make a living." Sometimes we discover that we have beliefs about being "lit up."

<u>What negative beliefs did you learn about shining your light and living lit up?</u>

Some examples: "Don't outshine me. That is dangerous. Are you sure you want to be doing that? You can't make money doing that. Who do you think you are?"

Sometimes we make rationalizations about what we love and block ourselves from ever letting ourselves be truly happy doing what lights us up.

I had a client who lit up like a sunbeam when he talked about adventure travel. He was a different being as he remembered how much he loved traveling and "getting lost with a friend."

He then shut down like a power outage when he started explaining that his love of travel was just an escape from his trapped childhood.

He also reflected upon a friend whom he had gotten lost with was now forbidden to travel with him anymore by his wife. He was starting to associate what he loved with restrictions and limitations. He was feeling punished for his love of travel.

<u>Take a moment to reflect on any "road blocks" you are aware of that keep you from living joyfully doing what you love:</u>

<u>Ask your heart what it wants you to do with these roadblocks?</u>

206

Change is possible.

It begins with awareness and then action.

When we become aware of that which is "not us" and things that need to be subtracted, we can begin to come home to our authentic self.

Using new self-loving practices, you can begin to choose to listen to your heart and take action to move beyond the roadblocks. You can create the life you want.

Being present to yourself and allowing **who you are to guide you**—

Being connected to **what you want** makes room for new possibilities for connection, safety and a lighter life journey.

Your light, love and passionate self are here in this moment—within you.

You can choose to be at home with your whole being—

You are able to think clearly—

You are able to feel your feelings—

You are embodied in your authentic shape–

Now you are able to sense and see the opportunities and vistas you couldn't see before.

Your compass is now in integrity with who you are and what you want.

Finale

Once we get a sense or glimpse of living lit up and following our heart, it's not easy to hide our light and get back in the old box.

Through our Inner Traveling we discover the freedom we seek.

We can emerge from the self-limiting, self-punishing, self-doubting, self-blaming, shame and addictions, that can keep us disconnected and living aimlessly or marching down paths that aren't where we wish to go.

Healing is possible and we can find our way back home.

Our life's trajectory depends upon how much we allow ourselves to:

BE WHO WE ARE and WANT WHAT WE WANT

In remembering who we truly are and claiming our gifts and heart's desires, we can reflect what is naturally ours. The light and natural essence of our passions that are within each of us.

Through this Inner Travel journey we find our very purpose for being here on this planet.

Why did I come to this life?

In this body suit?

With these gifts?

With this passion for?

Post Card Messages I Would Send

You have the LIGHT within you and you can connect and follow your Moyo.

Your heart will guide you to where your true north is.

Let your dreams and self-love be your guide and compass.

Inner Travel is much more interesting than any TV show you will ever see.

Your journey onward and inward is yours!

Being home within is the best place to be.

Enjoy your amazing life journey!

May your path be always lit from within.

Linda

Inner Travel Books for the Journey *(all available at Amazon.com or through author)*

A Princess And Her Garden, by Patricia R. Adson, Ph.D. & Jennifer Van Homer

Attitude Reconstruction, by Jude Bijou, MA, MFT

The Artist's Way Workbook, by Julia Cameron

The 5 Languages of Love, by Gary Chapman and Ross Campbell

Love Yourself, Live Your Spirit! by Sonia Choquette

Journey Into Love, by Kani Comstock *and her new book Missed Motherhood*

Eat, Pray, Love, by Elizabeth Gilbert

Compassion Haikus, by Karl Grass

Survivors Guide to Sex, by Staci Haines

The Dance of Anger, by Harriet Lerner, Ph.D.

The Emotional Incest Syndrome, by Dr. Patricia Love

Will I Ever Be Enough? by Maryl McBride, Ph.D.

Life Launch, by Pamela D. McLean and Frederic M. Hudson

Prisoners of Childhood, by Alice Miller now called - *The Drama of the Gifted Child*

Legacy of The Heart, by Wayne Muller

When Hope Can Kill, by Lucy Pappillon

The Wizard of Oz and Other Narcissists, by Eleanor Payson

Answering The Call, by John P. Schuster

The Power of Now & A New Earth, by Eckhart Tolle

Inner Travel Books for Love, Life & Work

These are just some of my favorite books & authors in the world!

Parenting:

The 5 Languages of Love of Children, Gary Chapman and Ross Campbell

Parenting from Your Heart, by Inbal Kashtan

Unconditional Parenting, by Alfie Kohn

Parenting from The Inside Out, by Daniel J. Siegel, M.D.

The Aware Baby, Helping Young Children Flourish, Raising Drug Free Kids Tears and Tantrums, all by Aletha Solter, Ph.D.

Nurture By Nature, by Paul and Barbara Tieger

Money/Leadership/Pets/Spirituality/Health:

The Wealthy Spirit, by Chellie Campbell

Man's Search For Meaning, by Victor Frankl

The Loved Dog, by Tamar Geller

You Can Heal Your Life, by Louise L. Hay

The Stop Walking on Eggshells Workbook, by Randi Kreger

Get Your Woman On, Presented by Kimber Lim

When I Was a Girl I Dreamed, by Margaret Baker & JP Matott

Take The Lead, by Betsy Myers

If It Were Easy They'd Call The Whole Damn Thing a Honeymoon, Jenna McCarthy

Constant Craving, by Doreen Virtue

Conversations with God, by Neale Donald Walsch

Travel Guides Who Helped Me Navigate My Way Home

Coaches, Healers, Teachers, Therapists, Astrologer

Ruth Ackerman

Pat Adson

Stacie Anthes

Carol Berg

Janie Bryan

Dr. Lynn Cantlay

Kani Comstock

John Walker Davis, *Energenesis*

Lisa Guerin and LT the horse named *Long Time Coming*

Staci Haines

Gayatri Heesen, *Acupuncture*

Dr. Gary Hubert, M.D.

Sharon Kennedy

www.HoffmanInstitute.org

Sudama Mark Kennedy

Carey Lindsey

Dr. Luc Maes, N.D.

Dr. Mark Mallinger

Pamela D. McLain

Ed McClune

Andy Milberg

Kathee Miller

Paul Schaffer

Alexander Tolken

Dr. Duncan Turner, M.D.

Jennifer Van Homer

Christy Walker
soulmap@earthlink.net

www.HudsonInstitute.com

I wouldn't be here now if it were not for you.

My gratitude & love to each of you!

Clients/Students/Colleagues/Co-Travelers

To all my clients, students, colleagues and co-travelers I have met along the journey, please know that your courage and commitment to heal and find your way home has inspired me and challenged me to keep learning and growing along the way.

Thank you for teaching me and allowing me to be a part of your path to wholeness.

Your light shines as a beacon for others!

Keep Shining!

Thank You Notes From Me

Dear: **Johnny, Jennifer, Jan, Annie J., Stacie A., Annie G., Alice, Kate, Wendy**

Thank you for your love, generosity and support of my dreams and passions!

Dear: **Tom, Jack, Karl, Mark, Pat M., Jennifer H., Tamar, Carrie, Toni, Pam, Kani, Shannon, Andi, Laurel, Mary, Barbara, Matt, Julie, Sarah, Laurie, Max & Rosie, Mac, Tricia, Julia, Trish, Emilia, Susan, John G., Dorian, Gary, Peter, Doug, Kimber, Liana, Lynn, Joanie, Bob, Relly, Deanne, Ross, Bill and Patty, Paul, David, Kevin, Rebecca, Linda D., Brett, Sudas, Nancy, Betsy, Chellie, Patty, Barbie, My dear beloved friends/family in Cast E 1982, West High Class of 1981**

Thank you for your encouragement, inspiration, guidance and enthusiasm!

Dear: **Newlin family and all my cousins, relatives and adopted family members**

Thank you for your love, prayers and for being the cheering squad!

Dear: **Annie J., Annie G., Wendy, Cris, Julie, Cecilia, and Over 40 Productions**

Thank you for your creative support and beautiful photography, graphics and filming of our music videos and Moyo: The Musical Journey Home

Dear: **Kate Wallace and Deborah Wynne**

Thank you for your musical talent and writing gifts you brought to the lyrics! Blessed am I to be partners in creating songs with you both.

Dear: **David West**

Thank you for your musical genius and mastery of producing. I am fortunate and blessed to have your guidance, wisdom, vast talent and treasures on this CD! My deepest gratitude for giving me a chance to create with you! Your studio is truly magical!

Your Travel Agent ~ Linda Newlin

Born into a military family, she lived in 10 places before she was 16. After graduating from high school, she was given the unique opportunity to travel and perform with the musical group Up With People, an international leadership and community service organization, visiting over 100 cities in a year including five countries, 26 states, and five provinces in Canada. Linda was awarded the ***Everyday Hero*** Award by the Up With People Alumni Association in 2012 for her community service work and support for organizations who are healing peoples' lives and her commitment to changing the world.

Linda is an entrepreneur, certified Hudson Institute Coach, keynote speaker, consultant, teacher, singer, songwriter, actress, activist, author and mother. She is also a coach and teacher for the Hoffman Institute USA, which provides a transformational process for individuals who are seeking to free themselves from the negative patterns learned in childhood and become the source of change in their own lives. www.HoffmanInstitute.org

She has worked with thousands of individuals in corporations, universities, non-profits and families who are courageously growing and moving toward their dreams and vision of positive contribution in their lives and in the world.

After receiving her Bachelor's degree in Communications from Pepperdine University, Linda worked for the American Express Co., Champlain College, and Pepperdine's Presidential Key Executive MBA business school. Since 1990, she has owned her own unique executive recruiting and coaching business focused on transition, integration, team building and personal growth.

She gives her time and treasure to organizations that are creating opportunities for dreams to come true–Community Film Studio of Santa Barbara is one–a pioneering community-based film studio giving once in a lifetime learning opportunities to anyone interested in acting or the business of making films. www.CFSSB.org

Post Cards From Inner Travelers

"Linda is a true teacher and spiritual guide who has impacted my family immeasurably for many years, and generations to come. Her timely insight, down to earth advice, earnest passion and sincere love are treasured by everyone she touches. Linda's counsel is a compass for the wandering soul."

- Max

"You have taught me to love myself and trust my spirit. You have an amazing gift to know when I need to be pushed and when I need to be nurtured. You are one of the most inspirational women in my life. I admire your passion and grace. I am very grateful to have you in my life. Your musical show and this book will make a huge difference in the world, as it has in my own life."

- Shannon

"I was so inspired by your Musical Show that I signed up for the Hoffman Process and after completing it. I feel so free, alive and present. Thank you for guiding me here so I could find inner peace, and begin my life anew. There are no words to express how grateful I am for your authenticity and inspiring words/message."

- Anonymous

"No more excuses, no more lies and pain! You sang those words and they permeated my heart and my head. I left the show and went home to end a long-term abusive relationship I have wanted to end for many years. Thank you for sharing your gift with the world. I will be eternally grateful for your passion and commitment to help people end their suffering and act in self-loving ways so the world can be a different place. My life is forever changed. Thank you!"

- Lorraine

"Linda has the gift of bringing her heart and wisdom to every meeting of souls. The love and acceptance she brings invites each of us to meet and love ourselves unconditionally. She sets the stage for freedom by giving each of us permission to be ourselves."

-A student who travels the light path and wishes to be anonymous

"As my coach, you inspired me to get my book written and provided me with insight, encouragement, and consistency…Your big heart, clear head and strong spirit kept me from dancing around what needed to be done. Your caring style was such a gift."

- Dina Washington, Author of **With Or Without You**

"Seeing your Show and hearing the lyrics made me go home and pull out a novel I started writing 25 years ago in college. Thank you for inspiring me to act now and stop waiting for something to happen."

- Phillip

"After seeing your musical show, I am going to try out for cheerleading next week and not be afraid. Thank you for inspiring me and reminding me that I can do it!"

- Angelina, age 8

"You have helped me move major blocks in my life so that I can be a free person and not be dragged down by the past. My life over the past three years has gotten better and better. Sometimes all I do is say, 'I need to call coach Linda and I just shift.'"

- Pat

"Linda helped me to transform my life. I've learned to trust myself, my feelings, my intuition and to speak my truth and own it. She guided me inward and now I love my whole self. I now can help others to see the truth and give birth to themselves."

- Nancy, Midwife

Credits of Love Your Self CD

LOVE YOUR SELF
 Linda Newlin – Vocal
 Barbara Coventry – Violin
 George Friedenthal – Piano
 David West – String Bass

LET MY GUARD DOWN
 Linda Newlin – Vocal
 Kate Wallace – Acoustic Guitar and Background Vocal
 Tom Ball – Harmonica
 Bobby Nichols – Drums
 David West – Electric Guitar, Slide Guitar, Electric Bass, Piano,
    Tambourine and Background Vocal

HEART LIKE A WHEEL
 Linda Newlin – Vocal
 Kate Wallace – Acoustic Guitar and Background Vocal
 Blaine Sprouse – Fiddle
 David West – String Bass and Mandolin

CRAZY MAKERS
 Linda Newlin – Vocal
 Kate Wallace – Background Vocal
 Jon Crosse – Saxophone
 Bobby Nichols – Drums
 David West – Guitar, Lap Steel, Electric Bass

OVER THE RAINBOW
 Linda Newlin – Vocal
 Jon Crosse – Saxophone
 David West – Acoustic Guitar, String Bass

IT'S NOT OKAY
 Linda Newlin – Vocal
 Jon Crosse – Soprano Saxophone
 Tom Lackner – Drums
 David West – String Bass

IF I HAD MY WAY
 Linda Newlin – Vocal
 George Friedenthal – Piano
 David West – String Bass

Credits of Love Your Self CD

SONG TO SELF
- Linda Newlin – Vocal
- Kate Wallace – Acoustic Guitar and Background Vocal
- Lorenzo Martinez - Congas
- Bobby Nichols – Drums and Tambourine
- David West – Electric Bass, Lead Guitar, Organ

I FORGIVE MYSELF
- Linda Newlin – Vocals
- Jon Crosse - Flute
- George Friedenthal - Piano
- David West – String Bass

TIME TO GO HOME
- Linda Newlin – Vocal
- Kate Wallace – Acoustic Guitar and Background Vocal
- George Friedenthal - Piano
- Bobby Nichols – Drums
- David West – Electric Bass and Background Vocal

LISTEN TO MY HEART
- Linda Newlin – Vocal
- George Friedenthal – Piano and String Arrangement

THE WOMAN I AM
- Linda Newlin – Vocal
- Kate Wallace – Acoustic Guitar and Background Vocal
- Lorenzo Martinez – Congas
- Bobby Nichols – Drums and Tambourine
- David West – Electric Guitar, Electric Bass and Organ

THIS LITTLE LIGHT OF MINE
- Linda Newlin – Vocal
- Kate Wallace – Acoustic Guitar and Background Vocal
- Tom Ball - Harmonica
- George Friedenthal – Piano
- Bobby Nichols – Drums and Tambourine
- David West – String Bass and National Steel

David West & Kate Wallace use only Elixir Strings

My gratitude and love to each of you! - *Linda*

More Credits of the Musical CD Love Your Self

**Love Your Self, Let My Guard Down, Crazy Makers, It's Not Okay,
Song to Self, Time to Go Home, The Woman I Am**
> Lyrics by: Linda Newlin (ASCAP) Music by: Kate Wallace (ASCAP)

I Forgive Myself
> Lyrics by: Linda Newlin (ASCAP)   Music by: Deborah Wynne (ASCAP)

This Little Light of Mine
> Public Domain, Arrangement by: Linda Newlin and Kate Wallace (ASCAP)

Heart Like A Wheel
> Anna McGarrigle (OBO Garden Court Music)

Over The Rainbow
> E.Y. Harburg and Harold Arlen (ASCAP)

If I Had My Way
> Jack Murphy & Frank Wildhorn (Bronx Flash Music/BMG Sapphire Songs)

Listen To My Heart
> David Ball & Allen Shamblin, Universal Music/Almo Music

Produced by: David West for PlayBall! Musical Services, www.DavidWest.com
Recorded by: David West, Studio Z, Santa Barbara, California
Mixed and Mastered by: Emmet Sargeant, Beagle Studios, Santa Barbara, Calif.
CD/Book Photography: Julie Hayes Nadler, www.JHNPhotos.com
CD/Book Live Performance Photos: Wendy Drasdo & Annie J. Dahlgren
CD/Book Graphic Design and Disc Photos: Annie Gallup
Book Cover Painting: Nancy Taliaferro

**For more information about coaching
or to book Linda for a speaking engagement/conference**

Please visit our websites

www.LindaNewlin.com

or

www.LunaMadre.com

**You can also purchase books, products, music, apparel,
DVD of Moyo: The Muziki Safari musical stage show**

At our on-line store at the above websites

New Inner Travelers™ Guidebooks

will be released later this year

Steadfast I Stand in the World
With Certainty I Tread the Path of Life
Love shall be in the depths of my being
Hope shall be in all my deeds
Confidence I shall impress into my thinking.

-Rudolph Steiner

A portion of profits from the sale of the CD:

Love Your Self: The Musical Journey Home

Will be given to organizations working to end abuse and to heal people so they can live their authentic, passionate and purposeful lives.

If you would like to be a sponsor and help gift and distribute this CD and the companion book to people in need, please contact us:

Luna Madre Music - Linda@LunaMadre.com

We are envisioning getting these to abuse shelters, rape crisis centers, Al Anon groups, domestic violence centers, etc.

If you would like to be an "angel" and support our dream Please reach out to us!

Thank you

Reprise

Self-Loving Practices for Inner Travelers™

1. Put myself first on the list

2. Resist my resistance

3. Work with a coach

4. Take time to meditate

5. Heal thyself

6. Forgive myself and others

7. Release vindictiveness

8. Apologize and allow others to apologize

9. Feel my feelings

10. Listen to my heart

11. Take action to fulfill my heart's desires

12. Allow myself to be happy at work and at home

13. Validate and acknowledge myself

14. Write love letters to myself

15. Be who I am and want what I want

16. Do what I love and shine my light in the world